INSPIRED BY TRADITION

INSPIRED BY TRADITION
THE ARCHITECTURE OF
NORMAN DAVENPORT ASKINS

TEXT AND PRINCIPAL PHOTOGRAPHY BY SUSAN SULLY

THE MONACELLI PRESS

CONTENTS

EDUCATED BY TRADITION

A leading figure in the present-day renaissance of traditional architecture, Norman Davenport Askins was also one of its earliest proponents. The architect launched his practice in Atlanta, Georgia, in the 1970s, when the lives and careers of the country's last generation of Colonial Revival architects, including Atlanta's Neel Reid, Philip Trammell Shutze, and James Means, had ended or were drawing to a close. The renewed interest in classical architecture was just beginning, fueled in part by the celebration of America's bicentennial. Preservation movements were gathering momentum, Colonial Williamsburg was "hot" again, and even ranch houses were beginning to sport columns, but thanks to academia's long allegiance to modernism, there was a dearth of architects with classical training or even a depth of knowledge of traditional architecture.

Askins describes himself as extremely fortunate to have arrived on the scene just as this void was being keenly felt. But his success and the value of his legacy are much more than the products of perfect timing. They are the result of a lifelong passion for traditional architecture and a determination to master its principles and details, despite the odds, and to demonstrate its enduring relevance in a body of work rooted in both the past and the present and likely to be cherished well into the future.

Although Askins, born in Birmingham, Alabama, in 1941, came of age in the modernist era, he was raised in the South, of which William Faulkner so famously wrote, "The past is never dead. It's not even past." His earliest memories are of family outings in the Alabama countryside, during which his parents pointed out old houses and told stories about their owners, prior and present. These trips often culminated at the home of his maternal grandparents, who lived in Eutaw, a small town well peppered with antebellum dwellings. His grandparents lived in one of them, an 1850s Greek Revival house that, though typically restrained in expression, was dignified by classical detail. Askins's memories of these visits are vivid—the enormous midday dinners, the gardens and greenhouse, the pilastered double privy, and the porch swing where his grandmother would sit, "all powdered up," on hot summer afternoons. And the lessons he absorbed were powerful: that classical design is timeless, that a good house is inseparable from its surroundings, that even the humblest outbuildings should be charming, and that houses are meant to be lived in—comfortably, companionably, and pleasurably—and enjoyed by generations.

As a boy in Birmingham, he began to take notice of his architectural surroundings, making daily visits with his dog Corky to nearby construction sites, where ranch houses were springing up like mushrooms. Studying their low-slung profiles, front-facing carports, low ceilings, and ugly windows, he compared them unfavorably with the nineteenth-century houses he'd come to admire. "Even then, I thought how much better they would have looked if they were a little more old-fashioned—my then-word for classical," says Askins. With the acquisition of a Schwinn Corvette bicycle, he expanded his sphere of study to other neighborhoods, where he refined his judgments and began to be able to identify architects by their designs.

"Before long," he recalls, "I was sketching floor plans and 'fronts' for fancy houses along traditional lines." Eventually, he took a course in mechanical drawing and secured a summer internship with his favorite Birmingham architect, Henry Sprott Long.

By 1960, when Askins entered the School of Architecture at Georgia Institute of Technology, the academic climate for a student inspired by history was not encouraging. Fortunately for Askins, the dean, Paul Heffernan, was an École des Beaux-Arts graduate who insisted on a foundation course in architectural history, and the school's library was filled with volumes on classical and early European architecture and monographs on nineteenth- and early-twentieth-century architects. Askins, a self-described "closet classicist" at the time, suspects that he was the first person since the 1930s to crack open the dusty folios on ancient and early European architecture. Although he paid necessary lip service to the modernist mantras being taught, when it came time to deliver his thesis, he came out of the closet, presenting hand-rendered plans for a new Alabama governor's mansion that was unmistakably classical in inspiration and detail. According to Askins, the faculty was speechless, but they gave him a passing grade and he escaped to Virginia, where attitudes toward the past were more congenial.

Accepted into the master's degree program in architectural history at the University of Virginia, Askins was "in heaven itself." His accounts of his time there are the ecstatic recollections of a man who has discovered his métier and his milieu. "I literally wallowed in the Virginia Piedmont for two years, taking Sunday road trips to see the sights, attending house auctions, and hunting down old houses I'd heard about," he recalls. Immersed in an academic setting where history was revered, he studied the evolution of classical and neoclassical architecture, reveled in a library containing books dating back to the eighteenth century, and learned to measure, analyze, and "read" old houses. After graduation, he secured a position at Colonial Williamsburg as an architect and architectural historian that offered even greater opportunity for the direct study of eighteenth- and nineteenth-century buildings. Askins's description of the field trips he and his colleagues undertook, led by Colonial Williamsburg's director of architectural research, Paul Buchanan, demonstrates the value of an education that includes first-hand study of historic architecture:

Mr. Buchanan knew everything there was to know about early Virginia architecture, but he rarely shared these pearls of wisdom. Rather, he encouraged us to "figure it out" for ourselves—thus, we never forgot our lessons. Off we would go to the countryside to see an "untouched house" he had discovered, and on arrival, we would be given an hour and a half to case it out on our own. The suggested sequence began in the basement and attic (Buchanan favored hiding places for recluse spiders and snakes), then on to the first and second floors, where we would try to pin down the original date of construction and the time sequence of later alterations and additions. How were the framing members connected? To what period did the nails date? Were the roof rafters numbered and installed sequentially? Were the mantelpieces original? Afterward, we reconvened to discuss the evidence we had found and offer theories, each of us hoping to be proven the best sleuth. Then we got back on the road to find the perfect country churchyard for bloody marys and a picnic.

Traveling abroad to attend the Attingham Summer School, Askins toured the great English

country houses with a faculty of renowned scholars and experts. His early travels also included visits to Europe and Greece, where he studied monuments he had hitherto seen only in books. The architect cites these opportunities to "touch, feel, and smell the real thing" as the key to designing houses in historical styles that not only look right, but also feel right. While he gained insights into the nuances of period detail, craftsmanship, and material, Askins says that his direct experience with architecture also taught him to play a little fast and loose with the canons. Houses like Drayton Hall that are pure expressions of a single period or style were unusual, he discovered. Less rare, but to Askins perhaps more compelling, were the houses that had evolved over time and contained intriguing clues about shifting tastes, technologies, and manners of living. He developed an eye for eccentric details that revealed the

quirks of untrained architects and provincial craftsmen, and a penchant for exuberantly eclectic landmarks like Villa Vizcaya in Miami, Beauport in Gloucester, Massachusetts, and Sir John Soane's house in London as expressions of personal visions and powerful imaginations. "It's important to be correct," Askins believes, "but it's even more important to know when to be 'incorrect.'"

Massachusetts-based architect Craig Douglas, who worked for Askins in the 1990s, explains the value of this observation-based philosophy: "Norman has an excellent sensibility about how to apply different aesthetic and design principles in the ways they were intended. Some architects become laborious and the architecture becomes heavy. Norman has a light touch combined with an instinct about when something needs to be technically correct and when you should

cheat to make it look right or add a touch of whimsy. That is really how it has always been done." This "instinct" is the product of an education that was, by necessity, undertaken largely outside the halls of academe. Tutored directly by primary sources—classical monuments, English country manors, eighteenth-century pattern books, early Colonial and antebellum Southern houses—Askins learned not just to imitate historical precedents, but also to think like the architects who created them.

While, in the words of another former staffer, Atlanta-based architect Ross Piper, Askins "can get down to the gnat's-eye level of detail," his biggest gift is the ability to master the essence of style. "If you can get that right," says Douglas, "there is room for play."

Every aspect of Askins's training was put to the test when he opened his practice in 1977. Early work

included a flurry of public and private preservation projects, many referred to him by Henry Green, the prominent Georgia preservationist and collector of early Georgia furniture. Among these were the preservation of Hofwyl-Broadfield Plantation in coastal Georgia, an 1806 rice plantation, now a Georgia state park, and the restoration of Atlanta's Herndon Home, the 1910 mansion built for Alonzo Herndon, a former slave who became Atlanta's first black millionaire. Residents of Atlanta's aging Colonial Revival houses began hiring Askins to renovate their homes, asking him to preserve their historic character while updating them for modern living. Askins found himself literally walking in the footsteps of Shutze, Reid, and Means, but he also quickly established his own identity, designing new houses in styles ranging from neoclassical American and English to French, Italian, and Mediterranean Revival. "I was the only kid on the block in the early days," says Askins, "so I had to be as flexible as possible, and that was the fun of it."

One of his first—and most entertaining—commissions was for a trio of "houses" for a goat named Billy T. Sherman, a pig named Ulysses S. Grunt, and a rabbit called Rabbit E. Lee. Recalling the pilastered double privy at his grandparents' house, he designed three diminutive outbuildings, which, while offering comfortable quarters for the animals, also complemented the Greek Revival plantation house of his clients—Senator Herman Talmadge and his wife. Askins is frequently praised for the charm of his outbuildings—dovecote-style garden sheds, vernacular English gatehouses, and a nineteenth-century-style carriage house that does double duty as a garage and rustic ballroom, but he is best known as the architect of commodious, lavishly detailed, and tastefully appointed houses that reflect an ever-broadening range of styles. A concentration of these are located in Atlanta's historic Buckhead neighborhood, but examples of Askins's work can be found along the coasts of Florida, Georgia, and South Carolina, in the Virginia Piedmont, the Kentucky horse country, and the mountains of North Carolina, as well as Chicago, Seattle, San Francisco, the western coast of Ireland, and Saint-Rémy-de-Provence.

Many of these dwellings are pitch-perfect homages to period styles, including an Atlanta residence designed in the early Federal style, with a Tower of the Winds portico on its restrained brick facade and neoclassical moldings, pilasters, over-door pediments, and fanlights within. Others are characterized by deliberate anachronisms intended to relate imaginary architectural narratives. One of the most elaborate of these is a French-style house in Atlanta with a half-timbered brick wing resembling a late fourteenth- or early fifteenth-century French farmhouse and a central block that appears to have been "gentrified" in the late eighteenth century with a baroque facade. Askins is inspired equally by classical, vernacular, and romantic architecture, including the Italian Renaissance country villas that informed the design of his own house in Atlanta, the hillside castles of the Dordogne that inspired a stone house in Cashiers, North Carolina, the Arts and Crafts architecture of Sir Edwin Lutyens, whose design for Homewood is echoed in a country house in nearby Highlands, and Dutch West Indian and Colonial Portuguese styles, melded together in a fanciful seaside retreat. Although each of these designs owes a debt to history, none are dogmatic or didactic.

This philosophy of approaching tradition with innovation and individuality—as well as an occasional touch of glamour and romance—is one Askins shares with the Colonial Revival architects who immediately preceded him. He is considered by many to be the bridge between them and today's new generation of traditional architects, including the principals of nearly twenty leading practices who trained in his office. But his roots reach back more deeply than that. "Askins has classical roots from a Southern point of view," says architect Yong Pak, a prominent member of Askins's professional offspring. "His work traces neoclassicism from the Colonial Revival back through early Southern architecture to its origins in England and Italy."

While shared vocabularies ranging from the classical to the vernacular unite Askins with predecessors dating from antiquity, his most vital link with the past is an understanding that architecture is not just an expression of the mind, or of aesthetics, or of a specific place and time, but also of the human spirit, which is timeless, multi-faceted, and filled with joy.

ELEMENTS OF TRADITION

In houses where the past and present coexist respectfully, all the elements are combined in a textured, layered way that creates an atmosphere of nuance and authenticity. Beyond their physical layout, such houses are defined by the way scale, proportions, craftsmanship, materials, and details work together on the senses and emotions to create an experience of harmony. During the beginning of the design process, it can be tempting to incorporate too many disparate ideas—things seen in magazines or on a recent trip—but unless the principles of appropriateness, logic, and continuity are applied, the result is a confusing jumble. Appropriateness, although it almost seems a lost term, is something I talk about frequently. It's essential to narrow down choices to the elements that matter most—a certain progression among interior and exterior spaces, use of a specific material, or even the proportions of windows. Then certain periods and styles are quickly eliminated, and others come forward for consideration. Once this happens, the parameters telling you what you can and cannot do in order to keep the house as pure as possible become evident. The fun part is knowing that once you've set the rules, you can also break them . . . as long as you do it the right way.

Logic is another word rarely applied to architecture, partly because we are no longer as concerned as we once were about the direction of the sun or the prevailing breeze. Before electricity, houses were designed to accommodate nature; now they can turn their back on it. I've found, however, that we still appreciate the effects when rooms are oriented to admit southern light and windows and doors are aligned for cross ventilation. Logic not only helps a house function better, it also makes it feel better. Logic should be applied to proportion, which is one of the most important factors shaping the way a room affects its inhabitants. When ceilings are too high, the feeling of wellbeing and intimacy are lost. The grand, tall rooms in English houses were meant to be ceremonial spaces—they're fine with fifty people in them, but with just two, they feel lonely. Unless you base proportions on the way a room will be used and what furniture is required, it will seem off balance. But it's also appropriate to play tricks with proportions occasionally in order to enhance architectural energy. The deliberate use of intentionally over-scaled or under-scaled elements can heighten the effects of a room. An over-scaled mantel in a small room increases its atmosphere of intimacy. A diminutive object placed at the end of a long vista seems farther away than it really is.

Continuity is an obvious factor in designing houses intended to evoke a particular period, place, or style. When every element, from the floor plan and materials to the tool marks of the craftsman, works together, the result is more than just an illusion—it's an authentic expression that is experienced in a very tangible way. But continuity is not the same thing as slavishness. Even when a house strictly adheres to period, it can still be appropriate to include a surprising departure or a purely fanciful moment. It was not at all unusual to find a Chinese room in a high-style Georgian house or a Spanish- or Moroccan-style smoking room in an Edwardian one. Inventing storylines that provide narrative logic for seemingly anachronistic or unexpected

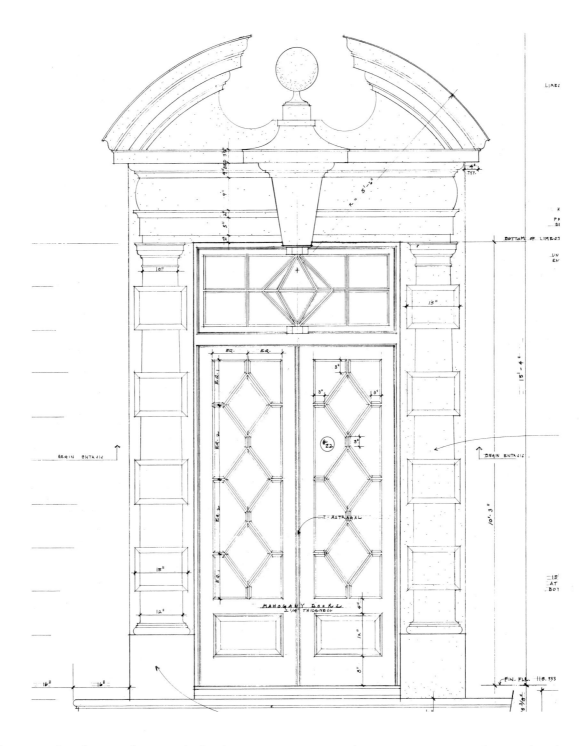

details is one of my favorite things to do for clients. One such narrative involved a marriage between an American heiress and an Italian aristocrat who, though impoverished, inherited gorgeous continental antiques. Although Italian in material and detail, the house "lived" with the relaxed informality of an American one, perfectly suiting my real-life client's Old World tastes and furnishings and modern-day lifestyle.

When it comes to employing the elements of tradition, the principles of appropriateness, logic, and continuity are important, but they can take you only so far. If a house lacks imagination, romance, intrigue, drama, and a little bit of fun, the design falls flat. Buildings that are informed by tradition need to be precise, but they also need to be as quirky as the people who create and live in them.

ENTRANCES AND DOORS

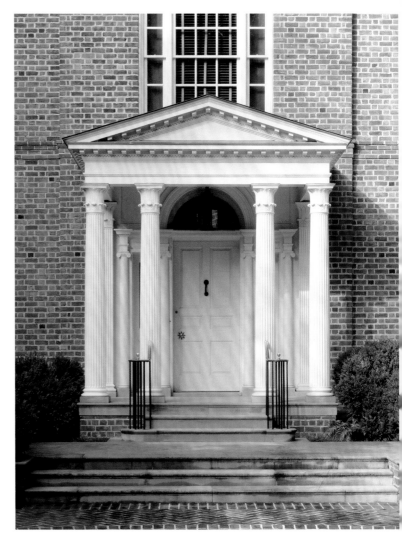

In even the simplest dwellings, the entrance seems to be the place where most architectural effort is invested. The pediment and the portico are two ways in which classical and neoclassical architects have drawn attention to entrances and made them more inviting and ceremonial. Porches, initially intended simply to provide protection from the elements, have also evolved into an important part of the ceremonial entrance sequence, especially in the South, where they immediately signal the style and character of the house. In finer dwellings, nearly equal attention is devoted to points of entry inside the house. Traditionally, there is a hierarchy, with the largest, most highly articulated entrances opening to the reception rooms. As you move away from the more public spaces, door openings decrease in height and width—a point lost on many homebuilders today. While they literally direct traffic through the house, doors also shape the emotional experience of passing from room to room. Although the placement of doors and openings is often dictated by logic, their arrangement can also be architecturally pleasing, allowing the varied spaces of a house to interact in a charming way. Sometime a false door that serves no purpose except to balance a room's symmetry and anchor furniture is as important as a working one. A sequence of doorways lined up to create an enfilade is one of a well-designed house's most generous gifts.

WINDOWS

Without question, windows are one of the most important elements in a house. Their shape, size, style, and number are immediately indicative of a specific period or region in architecture. When a client asked me to design a classical house with windows that came all the way down to the floor, any style prior to the late Georgian and early Federal periods was instantly eliminated. In houses built for northern climates, windows are fewer and smaller. Vernacular houses are much more likely to have irregularly spaced windows than classical ones. While continuity in windowpane size and proportion is essential, that doesn't mean every window has to look the same. Windows serve a variety of functions that affect their shape, size, and placement. Located in the center of a wall, they engage the view. Flanking it, they provide light and frame furniture and art. Very tall windows with elongated panes optically correct the height of a low-ceilinged room. In eighteenth- and nineteenth-century houses, interior windows became popular to lend light from one room to the next. Windows aligned to face other windows or doors have long been used to improve cross ventilation. Although today people tend to rely more on air conditioning, this arrangement offers balanced light and pleasing vistas. Once you have all the windows you need, more can be added in charming shapes and odd places. An elliptical window placed at the end of a long hall adds a terminating focal point. Dormers that don't line up perfectly or a quirky window punched out just where the light is needed on a dark stair add a human touch. Although symmetry is synonymous with the classical house, the effect can be stiff unless there is something slightly off-kilter or adding surprise.

18

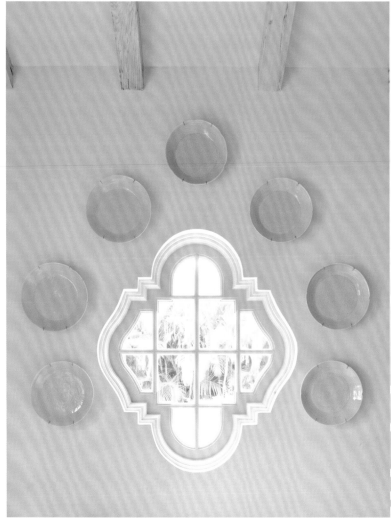

MATERIALS

No matter how perfectly correct the style of a house, unless it's constructed with the right materials, it won't look or feel authentic. The only way to know what materials to use and how to use them is to study period architecture first hand. Only then can you appreciate the subtlety and variety of materials employed, the way in which they were crafted, and how their appearance changes over time. Even when entirely appropriate materials are used, a house won't have any character or sense of soul if they look brand new. Salvaged terra-cotta tile or traditionally made reproduction tile in a variety of tones immediately adds hundreds of years to a roof, especially if you build in a little sag. Limestone blocks cut from the original stone face of a quarry provide a genuinely antique texture and appearance, but newly quarried stone can be aged by chipping or even blasting with water jets.

Materials also have a tremendous effect on the experience of the interior of a house. Antique wood and stone have a visceral quality that communicates not just through sight, but also by means of touch, sound, and even smell. Solid, genuine materials don't just look good, they feel good. A room paneled with old oak or hand-finished pine wraps its arm around you. Although marble and fine millwork are marvelous, a house can also be completely plain and absolutely superb. Shaker houses, bone-simple French and English cottages, or Italian farmhouses with nothing but plaster, wood, and terra-cotta have some of the most beautiful rooms you'll ever see. Ultimately, it's the honesty of materials that makes the difference between houses that are poor imitations and those that are rich and real.

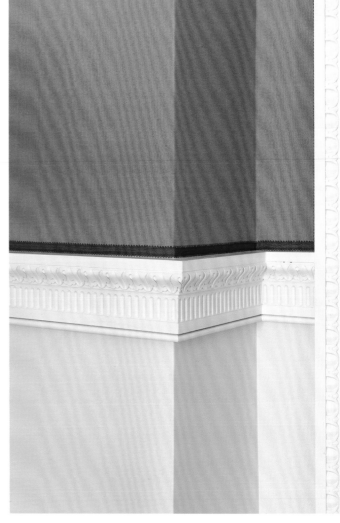

CRAFTSMANSHIP

Tool marks on wood and stone, brushstrokes on a painted wall, variations in plaster that has been hand mixed with pigment and over-troweled, steel that is pinned rather than welded, and mortise-and-tenon joints—these things talk to me. Even though other people don't always notice them, such signs of craftsmanship contribute a wonderful, soft, human character to a house. Wood with layers and layers of hand-applied finish literally increase the depth of a room, while slick sheetrock walls with gigantic, factory-milled cornices don't add a thing. There is nothing much more wonderful than a paneled room made of splined panels that shift in accordance with changes in temperature and humidity. Although they were nearly made extinct in the age of modernism, fine craftsmen who know how to make things artfully, using traditional tools and methods—and who are willing to take the time—still exist. It's well worth the trouble to track down stonecutters, ironmongers, plasterers who know how to create run-in-place moldings and medallions, and skilled woodworkers who can build mantels in period styles and methods and can piece together parquet de Versailles. Without master craftsmen like stair-builders who understand how to make a free-flying staircase float in a space or country carpenters who wield adzes, chisels, and handsaws, it's impossible to build a traditional house that is true to its source of inspiration.

22

DETAILS

Details are the jewelry of a room. They should be beautiful, unique, and carefully chosen. Unusual things, like a primitive piece of hardware or a hand-painted wood valance over a window, contribute an extra dimension that enlivens a space and gives it an almost human personality. Whenever you include a unique element, you deepen the soul of the house. In the pre-industrial age, everything was handmade and one of a kind. Once machine-made pieces became available, their novelty made them ubiquitous and even fashionable. It took a revolution—the Arts and Crafts movement—to bring back an appreciation for the quirky and the handmade, and then we almost forgot what we learned less than a century later. Occasionally, my clients and I go to Europe to search for everything from antique hardware and lighting to floors, paneling, furniture, and roof tiles. One purchase leads to the next, and sometimes a single shopping trip can end up reshaping the design of the house. On other occasions, a room calls out for a specific detail that's hard to find and must be custom fabricated, like the pair of hall tables inspired by drawings in *The Gentleman and Cabinet-Makers Director* by Thomas Chippendale that I had made by a master cabinetmaker. Although playing with the details can be fun, the principle of appropriateness still applies. Details should be added only where they belong, and should never looked contrived or pretentious. A tasteful woman never wears too much jewelry, and neither should a house.

VILLA VECCHIA

Atlanta, Georgia

Travel is essential to the development of an architect's taste and abilities. My wife and I have visited the Italian countryside many times, and perhaps because we're Southern, we have always been drawn to the way the homes there combine simplicity and comfort with understated elegance. Most of the rooms, except for a few on the principal floor, are extremely plain, with few baseboards or cornices. Their proportions, quality of light, and relationship to the surroundings seem to be much more important than ornamentation. Unlike urban Italian palazzos that are highly stylized and gentrified, the country villas are unpretentious and down to earth. Even when their scope and scale is grand, as at Posta Vecchia outside of Rome and Palazzo Terranova in Umbria, the materials and design remain humble.

When we decided to build a new house in Atlanta, I borrowed many ideas from rural Italian architecture. Much like the seventeenth-century baroque Villa Cetinale near Siena, the house includes a very compressed upper bedroom floor tucked beneath the deep overhang of a tile roof and a prominent engaged portico on the primary level, known as the piano nobile. Other than this grand neoclassical statement, the facade is minimally articulated, with plain windows, wooden shutters, and an absence of decorative detail.

But while the Villa Cetinale stands at the bottom of a hill, our house sits on top of one, where it might easily have overwhelmed the landscape. To tether it with ground-hugging elements, I copied a trick from Palazzo Terranova, dropping the entrance down a few feet and placing the front door midway between the raised basement and the piano nobile. This has the effect of minimizing the apparent height of the ground floor.

The exterior landing and split stair leading to it are also fairly low, a fact concealed by a closed balustrade that hides the landing and anchors the facade to the hill. Combined with an atypically high belt course, the low landing and front door create the impression that the piano nobile has a very high ceiling. It also provided sufficient height for the stucco portico, which, though intentionally over-scaled, is not overly complicated in expression. I spent two years tinkering with the proportions of the facade until I felt it was correct.

Similar illusions of scale are employed behind the house, where the focus is less on the house than a garden inspired by the grounds at La Foce in Tuscany. Although the villa at La Foce dates from the fifteenth century, its garden was redesigned in the 1920s by English architect Cecil Pinsent for well-to-do English owners. Grafting picturesque plantings inspired by Gertrude Jekyll onto a classical axial plan, Pinsent

created an aesthetic that I felt suited the Southern landscape and climate even better than that of Italy. Although the garden I designed is much smaller than the one at La Foce, its apparent size is exaggerated by Italian Mannerist devices, including a slanted lawn, skewed retaining walls, and steep steps that narrow as they approach a shallow upper terrace that seems higher and farther away than it really is.

As I designed the house, I imagined that it had been built in stages over a period of two or three centuries, like most of Italy's old villas. To make the living room resemble the primary room of a modest farm dwelling built in the early Renaissance, I gave it exposed ceiling beams, next to no trim, and archaic

leaded-glass windows inspired by the sixteenth-century Villa Piccolomini in Vicenza. The only architecturally important element is a massive limestone mantel inspired by a pair of mantels at Crane Cottage, an Italian Renaissance–style house built on Jekyll Island in 1917. As is often the case in Italian homes, richness in texture, pattern, and detail is provided by the furnishings rather than the architectural surroundings.

In contrast, the small sitting room in the front of the house features a deep cove cornice and the dining room is crowned by a handsome panelized ceiling inspired by the Italian gallery at the Detroit Institute of Arts. This shift in styles is intended to imply that the home's gentrified seventeenth-century residents added

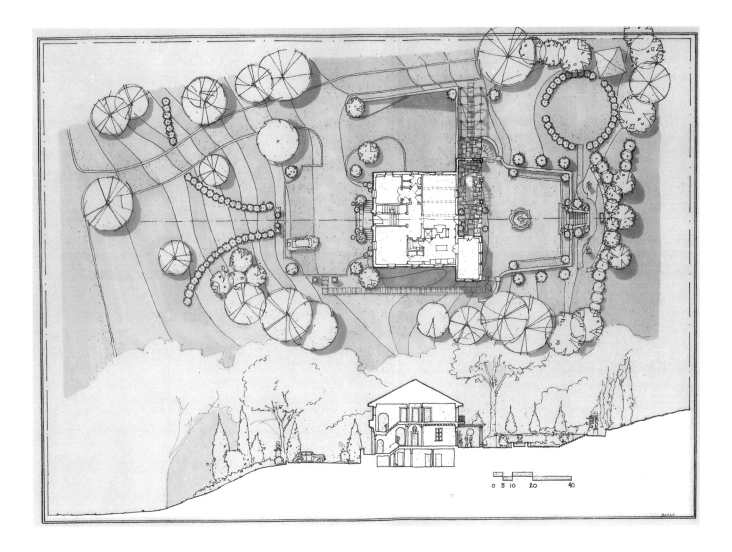

0 5 10   20   40

these front rooms to the "original" farmhouse, as well as a new facade featuring the neoclassical engaged portico. Decorative artist Jill Biskin, a former scenery painter for the Metropolitan Opera, deepened this storyline with a life-size portrait of those imaginary residents, reminiscent of fresco portraits seen in Palladian houses outside Vicenza. Framed by an arched reveal in the stair hall, the subjects of the portrait are dressed in period Renaissance clothing and bear a remarkable likeness to the house's present-day owners. Another portrait, this one a genuine seventeenth-century painting, hangs inside the front door beside a suit of arms complete with battle axe and pike. It's important to interject some fun when you build a

"historical" house to keep things from getting too serious and to avoid losing the quality of romance. If you lose that, then the house has no soul. A house is only as warm as the people who live in it and as romantic as their imaginations allow it to be.

OPPOSITE AND PRECEDING PAGES: The house resembles villas scattered throughout the Italian countryside. With stucco-over-masonry walls, casement windows, and barrel tiles combined with classical symmetry and an engaged portico, the facade recalls the country villas of the late Renaissance and early baroque period.
OVERLEAF: With an antique iron balcony off the master bedroom, a glazed loggia, and a pergola, the rear facade connects directly with the garden. For the most part, the plantings are dark green, interspersed with white and pink blooms.

ABOVE: The fountain is a married piece, with a quatrefoil basin
salvaged from Florida supporting a French garden urn with a classical
relief. Behind it, graceful stone steps rise to the terrace.
OPPOSITE: An axis runs through the center of the house from the front
door to the garden, where it continues, bisecting the fountain and
terminating at the top of the steps.

The living room furniture, textiles, and artwork convey the atmosphere of patrician country houses of the seventeenth and eighteenth centuries. Old master paintings and Flemish tapestries enhance the architectural elements— eighteenth-century tile floors, stucco walls, and hand-hewn pine ceiling beams of reclaimed barn wood. Windows of leaded restoration glass add more Old World elegance to the room. Standing lamps and an Italian iron chandelier illuminate the space.

ABOVE: In the dining room a paneled ceiling adds a sophisticated sensibility as does an Italian gilt-wood chandelier. Curtains with valances made from antique velvet vestments, a seventeenth-century Italian cabinet, and eighteenth-century Italian chairs complete the setting.

OPPOSITE: The master bedroom features an English neoclassical-style mantel flanked by doors made from painted panels salvaged from an Italian church.

OVERLEAF: The kitchen is handsomely furnished with a refectory table and an Italian chandelier. All the appliances are concealed in a pair of pantries, with the exception of the stove. Glazed double doors lead to the loggia, an informal dining and sitting room. Club chairs upholstered in gray-green velvet complement the collection of Chinese blue-and-white porcelain and an Italian painted cabinet.

RURAL ROMANCE
Athens, Georgia

Those who aren't familiar with architectural history often assume a new house built in a historical style should be seamlessly faithful to it—but the opposite is true. It's rare to find an old house that hasn't been remodeled at least once in its history. This is why intentionally creating rooms that seem to have been restyled and wings that look as if they post-date the "original" part of the house provides depth and a sense of history. As long as the architectural details and materials of each part are appropriate, the pieces work together in a way that is much more interesting and authentic than if the design adheres to a single period.

The central block of this residence appears to have been built in the mid-eighteenth century. Constructed of Tennessee fieldstone mixed with purplish-gray stone from Pennsylvania, the gambrel-roofed structure resembles the old farmhouses of the mid-Atlantic area. Although the mortar between the irregularly shaped stones is a lighter-than-expected shade of white, it is based on the burned-lime mortar used in the specific region and period that inspired the house's style. Other authentic details include the slate roof, twelve-over-twelve windows, and dormers that don't quite line up above the lower windows. By measuring a great many old buildings over the years, I

have learned that perfectly aligned elements are not always the rule.

The one-story weatherboard wing on the eastern end of the central block appears to have been added in the nineteenth century to provide more living space for a growing family. The stone entrance porch on the other side suggests an even later change, made at the turn of the twentieth century, when it became common to provide a side entry next to an automobile court. Inside the house, shifts in style and materials contribute more chapters to its imagined history. Refined moldings and details in the formal entertaining rooms imply that a second generation of residents, more affluent than their farmer parents, restyled the interior to reflect late eighteenth-century styles. The master bathroom, with its glamorous Elsie de Wolf–inspired details, including a mirrored-and-platinum-leaf vanity, is styled to date from the early twentieth century, when modern plumbing brought the luxury bathroom into vogue.

We designed this house more than twenty years ago with an intentional layering of historical elements. Fifteen years later, what first happened by design continued by circumstance, as the house changed hands, gained several additions, and underwent stylistic modifications. When the new owner asked us, in very twenty-first century fashion, to remodel the kitchen to

serve as the heart of the house, we added hand-adzed beams and painted board paneling to make it appear less kitchen-like and more like an extension of the adjoining family sitting room. In order to conceal clutter and intrusive appliances, we added a mudroom-style pantry resembling a slate-floored dairy repurposed for modern living. The current residents also requested a new room at the rear of the house where they could sit comfortably and enjoy views of the surrounding woods and fields. With steel-and-glass windows fitted between antique wood pillars, this new solarium resembles an old porch enclosed some time in the late twentieth century.

Recalling the moment she first stepped into the entrance hall, the current owner said she immediately noticed that the house not only looked older, but also felt older than it really is. She said that the sound of her footfall was different than it was in most other modern houses, a fact she attributed to the authenticity of this dwelling's materials and traditional craftsmanship. Because it is built with such integrity but also integrates what to the "purist" might seem an irreconcilable range of materials and styles, the house feels as genuine and uncontrived as one that actually has survived and evolved through centuries.

Built on top of a sunny knoll, this house was inspired by eighteenth-century farmhouses in the mid-Atlantic Piedmont. Pennsylvania and Tennessee fieldstone and shutters with a weathered finish add texture and color to the facade.
PRECEDING PAGES: A gallery extending more than sixty feet forms the spine of the house. The caned Louis XV sofa, with its faded blue cushions, has an air of relaxed elegance.
OVERLEAF: In the living room, Federal-style details include the custom-milled mantelpiece and crown moldings, while the Palladian-style window is more typical of the Colonial Revival, all suggesting the fictional remodeling of the house.

Weathered beams of reclaimed barn wood and painted board walls contribute old
farmhouse textures to the kitchen. With most of the appliances concealed in the
center island or the mudroom/pantry, the stainless-steel stove is the only element
of modern kitchen technology. The iron strapping and canopy-like shape of the
range vent were inspired by hoods seen in early twentieth-century houses.
Windows on either side of the sink bring light into room and bracket a slice of
wall that becomes a decorative focal point visible from the living room.

The heavily trussed ceiling of the family sitting room suggests that the space might once have been an old barn that was later refitted for residential use. This airy room is flanked by gardens and a pool terrace and terminates in a sunny garden room behind the fireplace wall.

ABOVE: A recent addition to the house, the gunroom features a chandelier with equestrian-style strapped leather and a leather-topped table studded with gun-shell butts. OPPOSITE: Rough-hewn barn beams and a broken slate floor create the impression that the pantry might once have been a dairy.

ABOVE: In the master bedroom, traditional bed hangings are juxtaposed with an antique French daybed and a Suzani coverlet.
OPPOSITE: The inspiration for the master bathroom's slab marble walls, sinks, and lavatories came from luxurious early twentieth-century American and English country houses.

FRENCH HISTORY
Atlanta, Georgia

When we were commissioned to build a new French-style residence in Atlanta, the clients made it clear that they wanted a home where they could live with their young children and entertain friends in an atmosphere of comfort and Old World charm. Wine connoisseurs who had traveled extensively in France, the client and his wife were enamored of the rural farming estates in the Loire, Burgundy, and Bordeaux provinces. We decided to begin the design process by studying this source of inspiration more closely, going to France with the clients, project architect Hoyte Johnson, and master builder Jerry Bonner.

Together we traveled the French countryside, touring old farming compounds, making notes and sketches, and also shopping for antique fountains, flooring, furniture, and lighting to integrate into the final design. Although there were many details that caught our eyes, the most important thing we learned was that almost none of these estates had been constructed within a single generation. Instead, they typically comprised a complement of structures built over several centuries, many of which were later updated in style, adapted for new uses, or joined together as families grew and prospered. It appeared that no matter how wealthy they became, French farming families never tore down the old structures on their land. They just built around them in the latest fashion.

This observation became the guiding idea behind the design of the new residence, which spans the crest of a wooded slope in the Sandy Springs neighborhood. When seen from the bottom of its cobblestone-edged drive, the house appears to be a late eighteenth-century baroque country manor with an elegant dressed-stone pediment and tower. As you follow the drive over a picturesque bridge, however, two more parts of the house come into view, both appearing to be much older and more primitive than the central facade. Constructed of half-timbered brick on a stone foundation, the north wing resembles a late fourteenth- or early fifteenth-century farmhouse with stables below and living space above. The south wing, which also looks as though it might once have been a freestanding dwelling, has the asymmetrical gable and off-kilter chimney typical of ancient vernacular French farm buildings.

Like the rural compounds that informed it, the house and its outbuildings are constructed largely from materials found close to home, including pale gold American limestone that closely resembles its French counterpart. While the majority of the exterior walls are constructed of roughly hewn stone, the facade also features dressed limestone details, including quoins, an arcade, and the baroque pediment that gives it a high-style flair. Once the exterior walls were completed, the masons chipped their surfaces and blasted them with high-powered water jets to give the recently quarried stone the appearance of age. The intentional sag in the roof's ridgeline—something we frequently saw in France but had a hard time convincing American roofers to reproduce—further adds to the house's apparent age. Terra-cotta chimney pots, irregularly spaced windows, and the uneven brick surrounds of the Gothic arches also contribute verisimilitude, as does the roof of clay tiles produced in a range of historically accurate colors and forms by Ludowici Roof Tile.

To capture the spirit as well as the appearance of an ancient French estate, we imagined a storyline beginning with a family of late-medieval farmers who built the half-timbered brick wing as the "original" structure on the land at the turn of the fourteenth century. When the farm prospered under the watch of another generation, the fictional family built a second farmhouse, now the master bedroom wing made of stone. Some time later, another house was built between the two, infill was added to connect them all, and a host of agrarian structures were constructed in the rear of the property. In the final chapter, when this family reached its apex of wealth and aristocratic prestige in

OPPOSITE, PRECEDING PAGES, AND OVERLEAF: Inspired by French farming estates built over several centuries, this house is designed as a formal central block flanked by more primitive structures, including a half-timbered brick service wing and a bedroom wing that evokes a vernacular stone cottage. These elements are unified by the materials, including limestone and variegated terra-cotta tiles.

the last decades before the French Revolution, they remodeled the central block of the house in the baroque style, adding a very fashionable facade in the center of the compound with an elegant suite of rooms behind, but keeping the rest of the structure intact. We even imagined latter-day modifications made when a twentieth-century family purchased the old estate and adapted it for modern living, stylistically updating the formal dining room and enclosing a rear arcade as a family room.

The design and materials of the rooms behind the baroque facade flesh out this narrative. In the foyer, the antique French limestone floor, ceiling with run-in-place plaster, and gilt-and-grisaille paneling inspired by a pair of Louis XVI over-door panels are pure expressions of late eighteenth-century French style. The library adjoining the foyer is faithful to the same period, with its handsome oak paneling, refined classical details, and carved marble mantel. As soon as you step into the lateral hall that runs between these "newer" rooms and the "older" ones at the rear of the house, the style begins to shift. With ceilings made of rugged hand-hewn beams that alternate with more refined plaster groin vaults, this transitional hall seems

to have only been partially gentrified. At the end of the hall sits a combination kitchen, family dining, and gathering space built with stone walls, hand-adzed beams, and antique clay tile floors reminiscent of many early French vernacular dwellings. The graceful stair at the opposite end of the house appears to be the product of a baroque-era remodeling.

Although several rooms are graced by ormolu sconces and crystal chandeliers, just as many have clay tile floors instead of marble, rough-hewn stone fireplaces, and forged-iron fixtures. Whether you are in the formal parts of the house or the most rustic ones, an intimate sense of scale, the presence of authentic materials, and evidence of the craftsman's hand create

an atmosphere of warmth and charm. The owners love it when people describe their house as cozy, because the quality of intimacy in the midst of grandeur is what they admire most about the French country dwellings that inspired them and wanted to evoke at home.

ABOVE: Designed in the style of a late-medieval farmhouse, the carriage house wing features half-timbered brick walls, dormer windows, board-and-batten shutters, and an overhanging second story.
OPPOSITE: The facade of the central block incorporates a classical arcade, symmetrically spaced windows, and dressed-limestone pediment. The gas lantern that marks the entrance was acquired in France.

Outbuildings, designed in an agrarian vocabulary with irregular rooflines and brick trim,
surround a small courtyard with an antique terra-cotta fountain in the center. In the motorcourt,
a French fountain originally intended for watering horses adds to the rural atmosphere.

As the ceremonial entrance of the house, the foyer gives an impression of formality, but its soft palette and intimate scale are welcoming. Eighteenth-century overdoor panels inspired the palette of grays highlighted with water-gilded trim, ormolu sconces, and a crystal chandelier.

Combining groin vaults and rustic ceiling beams, the long hall that runs through the house is both grand and rustic. European furniture, sconces, and tapestries are reminiscent of the furnishings of an eighteenth-century French manor house.

The broad steps of the gracefully curving stair ascend through the bedroom wing. The hand-wrought railing features cast-bronze rosettes and stylized lily-of-the-valley—one of the client's favorite flowers. Tall French windows overlooking the terrace and a bull's-eye window above bring in natural light. OVERLEAF: In the family room, hand-hewn posts and beams are juxtaposed with modern steel-and-glass windows that frame views of the courtyard.

Across the courtyard from the family room is a covered porch furnished
with casual rattan seating furniture. Hand-hewn oak beams support
the terra-cotta roof tiles above an arcade of dressed limestone columns.
At the center is an eighteenth-century French chimneypiece.
OVERLEAF: On the rear of the house, the kitchen and family room wing,
with the thick stone walls of a northern European farmhouse, contrasts
with a covered terrace inspired by the architecture of southern France.

CLASSICAL GRACE
Atlanta, Georgia

These clients presented us with a vision of a dwelling that combined the beauty and integrity of historic architecture with the qualities of warmth, dignity, and soul.

Longtime admirers of Southern architecture, they were especially drawn to the stone houses of the North Carolina and Virginia Piedmont, where Georgian and Federal precision met the earthiness of native stone. Like people who look good in black tie or blue jeans, houses like these can be dressed up or dressed down, allowing you to live in them however you like. As a source of inspiration, they provided the perfect starting point for our design.

The main block of the Federal-style residence is a classic five-bay, two-story house, clad in gray fieldstone that imparts elegance and gravity to the facade. As is often seen in mid-Atlantic structures, large stones are placed as quoins at the corners of the structure to insure stability, and smaller, more irregularly shaped pieces form the infill. In contrast to the masonry's robust, masculine character, the central block's base of dressed limestone is neatly tailored, and its Federal details, including a portico with slender, tapered columns and a Chinese-Chippendale balustrade, are almost feminine.

Unmatched wings ramble off on either side of this symmetrically arranged building, one resembling a kitchen house and the other, a garden pavilion with a whimsical, bell-shaped copper roof. Both appear to have been joined to the main block at some point after their construction with weatherboard hyphens, a common feature of old country houses that have evolved over time.

One of the qualities the owners admired most about the historic farmhouses in Virginia and North Carolina is the care with which they are situated in their surroundings. They wanted their Atlanta house to have that same quality of inevitability and belonging, and landscape architect John Howard played an important role in evoking it. Celebrating the old trees on the gently sloping lot, including two beautiful oaks near the front of the property, he created a bucolic setting resembling the well-tended park of a country estate. The graceful driveway curves through stone posts and a picket gate before ending beside the house, creating the impression of motoring up to a house in the country rather than parking before a suburban residence. A flagstone path that winds between the house and the lawn, beside trees and between plantings

of boxwoods before ending at the foot of the portico, prolongs enjoyment of the natural setting.

Endowed with high-style Federal detail, the entrance hall is more formal than the fieldstone exterior suggests. Marble parquet covers the floor, Doric columns frame a glimpse of the living room at the end of the hall, and a casement with a neoclassical pediment opens to the adjacent dining room. The most dramatic feature of the entrance hall is a large spiral stair with a shapely mahogany rail and an iron balustrade with oxidized bronze rosettes. On the second-floor landing, a tall circle-head window frames a view of the front lawn and a screen of Ionic columns marks the entrance to the bedroom areas. A gracious center hall featuring a beautiful spiral stair was among the first requests of the clients, but interestingly, the idea originated with their son when he was a boy. Years earlier, he told his mother he wished their home at the time had a central stair hall, which in his view formed the heart of a house. Out of the mouths of babes come pearls of wisdom— especially if they're Southern.

In keeping with the overarching vision of charm and livability, every time we introduced a formal element, we found a way to take it down a notch, warm it up, or give it soul. For example, instead of using white and black marble for the entrance hall floor, we chose an ivory field with chocolate brown borders and cabochons. In the dining room, where an oval ceiling reveal and an Adamesque medallion epitomize late eighteenth-century elegance, French doors with transoms replace more typical double-sash windows, forging an easy relationship with the natural surroundings. Like the dining room, the living room has a wall of French doors that overlook the pool terrace, toning down the classical elegance of Doric columns, pilasters, and a Georgian mantelpiece. These openings frame views of the pool and gardens, a pool house resembling a Roman arcade, and a pair of symmetrical wings with matching pediments.

OPPOSITE, ABOVE, AND PRECEDING PAGES: A gently sloping piece of land with a pair of mature oak trees is the ideal setting for a house in the style of a Federal-era stone farmhouse. The house is large, but it appears welcoming rather than imposing. Tall windows and doors visually reduce the size of main block, and a collection of low wings and outbuildings provides living space without expanding the central mass. Deliberately distinct from each other, the wings read as though one was originally a detached kitchen building and the other a garden pavilion. Vernacular materials, including fieldstone and painted weatherboard, relax the formality of the massing.

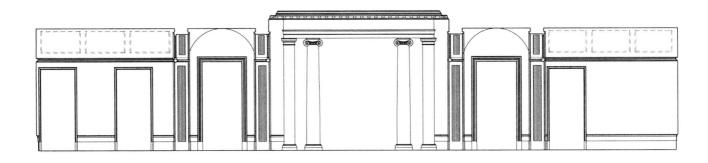

The plan of the house and its outbuildings is highly ordered, with a transverse axis bisecting the property from the portico to the pool house and a longitudinal axis formed by a pair of identical corridors that connects the stair hall to the rooms in the side wings. The long corridors are enlivened with barrel-vaulted ceilings and casements with Federal-style millwork and circle-head transoms. Although this axial plan is a very formal device, it accommodates a natural flow among the entertaining rooms and more relaxed family areas, as well as between indoor and outdoor spaces.

The pool terrace and gardens can be seen from the front door and are just a short step down from the level of the living room and most of the other rear-facing rooms. Walking outside, one immediately feels the embrace of the two low wings that define a protected courtyard for family life and entertaining.

Although this courtyard is completely symmetrical, stone walls of varying heights, a English-style potting shed, and a kitchen garden with a picket fence add charming irregularity along the perimeter. Balancing the rigor and refinement of the floor plan and decorative details, these rustic, rambling features reveal the softer side of the house, inviting its owners to live in it however they like.

PRECEDING PAGES AND ABOVE: Doric columns crowned by a blind entablature create an imposing entrance into the receiving room. Symmetrically placed doorways with deep cases and fanlight transoms open to hallways that lead to the family's private rooms.
OPPOSITE: Simultaneously graceful and stately, feminine in form but masculine in detail, the stair expresses what the clients refer to as "the multiple personalities" of the house. The stair has a gentle riser ratio, an iron balustrade with cast bronze rosettes, and a robust handrail based on English precedent.

The generous proportions of the Federal-style pediment at the dining room entrance balance the grandeur of the stair. The ceiling is detailed with a large elliptical reveal and a Robert Adam–inspired plaster medallion. In contrast, the French doors have simple transoms and surrounds that focus attention on views of the lawn and trees. Green strié walls provide a backdrop for the decorative details and reinforce a sense of unity with the landscape.

ABOVE: A circle-head window with graceful millwork and the classical details of an Ionic screen carry the architectural energy of the entrance hall up to the second floor.

OPPOSITE: The living room, located between the entrance hall and the rear terrace, functions both as a place for gathering and for circulation. A Georgian mantel anchors the only large expanse of wall uninterrupted by doors and openings.

OVERLEAF: Based on an English precedent, the oak paneling in the library was constructed in the eighteenth-century manner with splined wood panels that shrink and expand without buckling. A custom-designed mantelpiece combines a handsome Georgian silhouette with delicate egg-and-dart molding.

ABOVE: With thick stone walls, a tiled roof, and timber outriggers reminiscent of English vernacular outbuildings, the potting shed becomes a folly that breaks up the symmetry of the gardens behind the house.

OPPOSITE: On the rear facade the elliptical window and second-story porch echo the Federal elegance of the entrance facade, but the two rear wings are vernacular in style and reduced in scale. The U-shaped arrangement accommodates indoor-outdoor entertaining as well as a private area for relaxed family recreation.

DESCANTE
Atlanta, Georgia

The best houses are reflections of the people who live in them. The clients who commissioned this residence—scriptwriters who moved from Hollywood to Atlanta after long and successful careers—have great style, big imaginations, and a huge sense of play. They wanted "an exciting classical house," filled with interesting details and delightful surprises—as well as plenty of space for visiting children and grandchildren, large parties, and charity events.

Given their careers and their personalities, it was no surprise that they were very active in the design of the house and a fount of ideas, like concealing plumbing in a kitchen wall in order to grow herbs and vegetables indoors. At one point, the couple, who owned a vineyard, considered installing a miniature train in the vast basement to deliver guests from one end of the wine cellar to the other, with stops along the way at areas designated for Burgundy, Bordeaux, and other wine-producing regions.

If many of their ideas proved too fanciful, those suggestions imbued the design process with a powerful sense of play and imagination. The clients had a significant impact on the house when they began shopping at auctions and in Europe, sending back shipping containers full of architectural artifacts to be included in the design. One day, they called from France to tell me they had just purchased the facade of the house. This seventeenth-century limestone facade with carvings of grapes and vines turned out to be too small for the house but perfect for the pool pavilion. Executed with a touch of rustic primitiveness, its steep pediment and shallow carvings are charmingly naïve and lend both elegance and whimsy to the pool terrace.

For the primary facade of the house, project architect Yong Pak and I designed an impressive confection of Italian architectural virtuosity. An engaged portico with cut limestone pilasters and a tall entablature is surmounted by a window with a shapely broken cornice. Above that, a pair of pumped-up volutes and a pediment ornamented with a shell motif provide more accents of baroque exuberance. The facade is primarily inspired by Italy's baroque churches and palazzos, but it also takes cues from Florida's Mediterranean Revival architecture, especially Villa Vizcaya, which we studied as we developed plans for the house. These lavish American palazzos from the 1920s and 1930s provide a rich trove of ideas that invoke a bygone era of gracious living and lavish entertaining.

The central block of the
front elevation is enlivened
by a highly articulated
projecting mass crowned by
a pedimented pavilion
flanked by baroque scrolls
resting on the main cornice.
Drawing from ecclesiastical
rather than residential
precedents, this facade
creates a dramatic initial
impression. In contrast to
the front elevation, which is
essentially flat, the rear
facade is relieved by a pair of
projecting two-story wings
that define a central exterior
room wrapped by the house's
primary entertaining and
circulation spaces.

95

The facade makes a monumental first impression, but the rooms behind it feel inviting, rather than intimidating. Unfolding like a novel, the floor plan keeps you guessing about what will happen next. Instead of opening directly into the entertaining rooms, for example, the entrance hall terminates in an arched doorway that leads to a cross hall and frames a view through French doors of the courtyard behind the house. Inspired by the arcades at Villa Vizcaya, this lateral hall has ribbed groin vaults, limestone pilasters, and leaded-glass doors with scattered panes in shades of lavender and rose that my clients refer to as "confetti glass." Romantic in the extreme, this space is also completely practical, tracing a straight line from the rooms on one end of the house to the other. On either end of the long hall, the living and dining rooms open

to the courtyard with floor-to-ceiling French doors, which can be opened to transform the rear of the house into a single large entertaining space.

The largest rooms in the house include a neoclassical living room featuring Temple of the Winds columns and pilasters, a paneled dining room, and a Renaissance Revival–style paneled library. Although these rooms are grand in scale, their unified proportions

ABOVE: Hidden from the street, the house is approached by a winding drive that opens into a wide forecourt accented by an antique fountain purchased by the clients in France.
OPPOSITE: Figural stone corbels, found in the Marché aux Puces in Paris, support antique cast-iron balconies. The chessboard pattern of contrasting limestone squares in the courtyard was one of the clients' fanciful ideas.

keep them from feeling cavernous and the patina of antique stone and wood softens their impression. The house also contains several priest-hole-like spaces and concealed passageways, such as the "Romeo and Juliet" staircase to the master bedroom hidden behind a Gothic-style panel. Nearly every room contains one or more of the artifacts the clients purchased while shopping for the house. Although some of these challenged us at first, they ultimately provided opportunities to think as inventively and creatively as possible. Not everyone will notice the way we mounted a stone fleur-de-lis above a door in the library and framed it with a broken entablature, but nobody forgets the powder room. As soon as you enter, water begins to spout from the human face of an elaborately carved armorial escutcheon into a monumental classical urn purchased from the Jack Warner estate.

The couple we designed the house for named their home Descante—the Italian word for an ornamental, improvisational melody sung in counterpoint to plain song. The essence of the word is that you are not simply singing along with the tune, but that you are doing so in your own individual way. A perfect description of the clients and their house, this quality also appeals to the current owners. At first, this couple wondered whether it might be too much house for just two people, but their fears were unfounded. Descante had become one of Atlanta's favorite charity event destinations even before its construction was complete, and its rooms are rarely empty. As the current owners say, "This house is meant to be shared."

PRECEDING PAGES, LEFT, FROM TOP LEFT: A limestone niche at one end of the hallway; over-scaled brass lanterns focus attention on the fine plasterwork of the groin vaults; antique oak parquet de Versailles in the living room; a broken entablature in the library with a French architectural fragment.
PRECEDING PAGES, RIGHT: In the gallery across the rear of the house, arched openings filled with leaded glass address the courtyard. With cut-limestone pilasters and run-in-place plaster ribs and corbels, this hall is one of the most intricate spaces in the house.
RIGHT: The demi-octagonal library is paneled in northern white pine that resembles both English deal and the cypress favored by Florida's Medi-terranean Revival architects.

ABOVE: A monumental stone urn replaces an ordinary lavatory in the
powder bath. When the room is entered, water from a bronze
spout in the escutcheon mounted on the wall splashes into the urn.
OPPOSITE: Corner cabinets crowned with roofs of antique tile
add a touch of fantasy to a kitchen with roughly textured plaster
walls and antique French terra-cotta floor tiles.

The quirky details of a seventeenth-century French limestone facade, including an overly steep pediment and primitive carvings, suggest the work of a rural French craftsman. Relief carvings of grapes and vines imply that it might once have graced a vineyard. Vestiges of this architectural relic are incorporated into the pool pavilion.

THISTLEWAITE
Highlands, North Carolina

Almost everyone who knows architecture loves Homewood, the country house English architect Sir Edwin Lutyens designed for his future mother-in-law, the Dowager Lady Lytton, in 1901. There is something so welcoming and friendly about its steeply pitched gables, upswept eaves, sturdy brick chimneys, and the way it engages the surrounding gardens and landscape. When I received a commission to design a house in Highlands, North Carolina, with a strong garden focus, I thought of Homewood immediately—as had the clients. They didn't want a mountain house that was all bark shingles and rustic timbers or a modern one with soaring ceilings and picture windows. Instead, they envisioned a sophisticated house marrying the charm of an English garden cottage with the vernacular traditions of the Blue Ridge Mountains. Lutyens's fascination with England's rural architectural past, his genius for reinterpreting it for modern country living, and his understanding of how to integrate houses with their setting provided a perfect source of inspiration.

Similar to the English vernacular houses that Lutyens loved, the first cottages in the Highlands area were constructed of indigenous materials. Even when finer products became available, the local builders preferred to work with native wood and stone, inventing a picturesque mountain architecture in the process. Thistlewaite, the name my clients gave their house, follows this tradition by employing mostly local material in its construction. The exterior walls are clad with slab wood cut from blighted hemlocks felled on the property, and its porch pillars and massive fireplaces are made from stone found on site. The house's U-shaped plan is a direct reference to Homewood's garden elevation, where two projecting wings define a semi-enclosed courtyard, accessed from several ground-floor rooms and visible from many windows. Other than the twin peaks of its gable ends, however, our design does not resemble Lutyens's English Arts and Crafts–era country house.

Unlike Homewood, which is approached by a drive proceeding straight to the front door, Thistlewaite has a roundabout entrance sequence. Its driveway curves and crosses a creek over a humped stone bridge before terminating beside one of its gable ends. Other than a pair of carriage house–style garage doors, there is no entry point on this side of the house. To reach the true entrance to the house, you first must follow a flagged path around the side of the house and pass beneath a lychgate with a fanciful antique zinc finial. The round shape of the gate's stone arches combines with the dip of its high doors to create a circular oculus that frames a beckoning garden vista.

With a stone terrace, a lawn enclosed by a low rock wall, borders of shrubbery and flowering plants, and a courtyard parterre, the garden designed by landscape designer Alex Smith, in collaboration with the clients, unfolds in a sequence of room-like spaces. The terrace functions as an outdoor dining room complete with a fireplace, and the parterre, with its patterned planting of groundcovers, resembles a foyer

adorned with an Oriental carpet. The wings flanking the courtyard offer sheltered porches—one serving as the master bedroom's open-air sitting room, the other as a covered passageway to the front door. This passageway parallels an all-season living area that resembles an old stone porch enclosed at some point in its history with large casement windows.

With a sitting area decorated with antiques, comfortably upholstered furniture, and a dining table beside a massive fireplace, this versatile porch-style room is one of the most well-used spaces in the house. The large kitchen next door, with which the fireplace shares a chimney, is equally inviting. Like the porch, it is a multi-purpose space, with areas for cooking, sharing meals, and enjoying morning coffee by a fire in the raised hearth. The fireplace, decorated with a radiating pattern of slate loosely based on a Lutyens design, is one of many unusual details that contribute to the house's appealingly eccentric character. Other unique elements include circular windows cut into the wall between the dining room and entrance hall, which frame bronze medallions with a thistle motif that inspired the name of the house.

PRECEDING PAGES: A winding flagstone path leads around the side of the house to a rural English-style lychgate. The slightly over-scaled zinc finial, acquired by the clients, heralds the tiny structure as the ceremonial entrance to the house.
ABOVE: In typical Arts and Crafts style, the primary facade combines primitive materials and craftsmanship with subtle sophistication.
OPPOSITE: The arched opening of the gate frames a strategically placed golden honey locust.

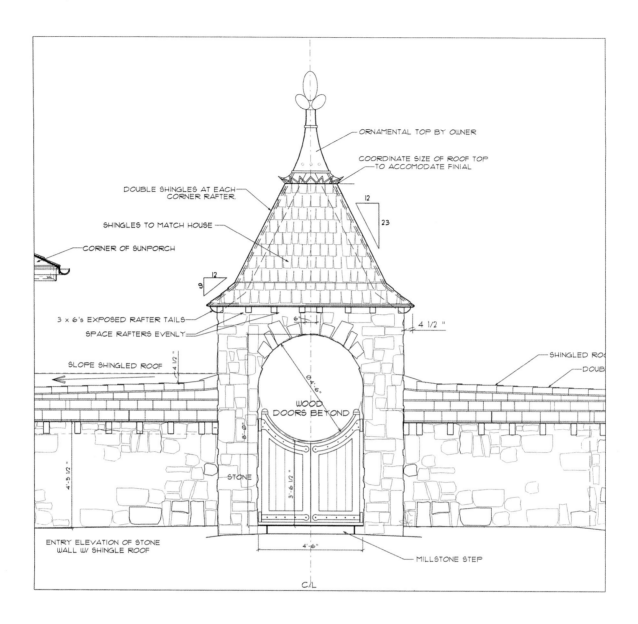

ORNAMENTAL TOP BY OWNER

COORDINATE SIZE OF ROOF TOP
TO ACCOMODATE FINIAL

DOUBLE SHINGLES AT EACH
CORNER RAFTER.

SHINGLES TO MATCH HOUSE

CORNER OF SUNPORCH

3 x 6's EXPOSED RAFTER TAILS

SPACE RAFTERS EVENLY

SLOPE SHINGLED ROOF

WOOD
DOORS BEYOND

STONE

ENTRY ELEVATION OF STONE
WALL W/ SHINGLE ROOF

MILLSTONE STEP

SHINGLED ROOF

DOUB

4 1/2 "

4'-6"

C/L

Found by the clients, these were salvaged in Brussels and are believed to have been foundation ventilation grates.

Like most of our projects, Thistlewaite was the product of collaboration among its creators, including the owners, the landscape designer, project architects Hoyte Johnson and Brent Mooneyham, interior designer Jackye Lanham, and the builder Tommy Chambers and his team of master craftsmen. A hoarder of salvaged building material, Chambers brought old timbers and barn wood to the site that deepen texture and patina. Lanham suggested dressing up the dining room with a gold fillet and lightening the kitchen's mood with a striped, painted floor. And the owners, who collect antiques and are aficionados of architecture and the decorative arts, played a very active role in design. That's what makes the house so magical. Like Homewood, it's a deeply personal country house that combines imagination with authenticity and comfort with charm.

An English vernacular-style lychgate is the ceremonial entrance to the house. Opening to a series of outdoor rooms, it leads to a flagstone path that directs traffic to a front door located beneath the shelter of a projecting porch.

Large windows fitted between stone pillars suggest an old fieldstone porch converted for year-round use. The flagstone floor and weathered wood ceiling reinforce the impression. When open, casement windows dissolve the boundaries between the room and its natural setting.

Hand-adzed beams and boards salvaged from nearby barns contribute vernacular character to the living porch. The dining area is heated in cool months by blazes in the massive fireplace. Built of granite found on the property, the wall-sized chimneypiece has a huge stone mantel and shelves where the clients display a collection of Southern pottery.

A raised hearth warms a kitchen sitting area. The graphic fireplace surround is executed in slabs of slate, with a niche below the hearth for wood storage.

OVERLEAF: Designed for family cooking and entertaining, the kitchen combines efficiency with style. Modern appliances are hidden in adjacent pantries, allowing more counter space and wall-mounted cabinetry, including a decorative shelf where a collection of antique pewter is displayed.

117

ABOVE: With flagstone floors, a wide door made of wormy chestnut,
and large windows, the front hall feels like a shaded walkway.
The change from the stone floor to the polished wood
of the living room and the dining room marks the transition from
the casual, summery parts of the house to the more formal rooms.
OPPOSITE: Placing a round table in the center of a square dining room
creates intimacy as well as easy circulation through the space.
A recess between two windows accommodates an antique sideboard.

A partition wall with a wide segmental arch separates the dining room from the front hall. Two round interior windows bring light into the room and frame a pair of antique bronze medallions with a thistle motif collected by the clients. A warm shade of green complements the natural setting and the collection of antique English transferware. A thin gold fillet beneath the crown molding adds a touch of English country house formality.

PRECEDING PAGES: The living room showcases the clients' collection of
English, Scottish, and American antiques. Although the beaded wood
paneling is humble, a satiny paint finish makes the room more formal, as do
curtains with elegantly trimmed valances and a handsome mantelpiece.
ABOVE: A Gothic arch opening adds a touch of whimsy to the master bathroom.
OPPOSITE: Built-in shelving in the passageway connecting the living room with
the master bedroom displays a collection of early miniature furniture.

ABOVE: Steeply sloped ceilings, country antiques, English china, and an old-fashioned lavatory add charm to one of the upstairs bedrooms.
OPPOSITE: In the upstairs hall, one wall is lined with bookcases lit with old-fashioned library lamps and the other is hung with a framed collection of pole screen shields.

MODERN ENGLISH

Atlanta, Georgia

Created with the active collaboration of a couple whose tastes were formed by two different traditions, this house offers a fresh, contemporary approach to classic style. The husband, a native of Atlanta, had recently inherited a collection of furniture acquired by generations of his Southern family and wanted the new house to provide an appropriate setting for them. The owner of several hardwood forest products companies, the husband also envisioned showcasing a variety of wood species and fine millwork in the house. His wife, a native of Norway, came to the project with a more pared-down, Scandinavian sense of style. She envisioned a light-filled, minimalist interior with a neutral palette and restrained detail. Designed by a team that included project architects David Stoll and Hoyte Johnson, interior designer Anne Whitman, and landscape architect Richard Anderson, this house is a synthesis of old and new, reflecting Southern, English, European, and Scandinavian sensibilities in a true crossroads of design.

The exterior is drawn from the late nineteenth-century English Arts and Crafts aesthetic defined by C. F. A. Voysey and his contemporaries. While complementing the romantic Tudor Revival houses in the surrounding neighborhood, the style is also bolder and more inventive. The architecture includes archaic elements, including massive multi-flue chimneys and stone gatehouses, but the geometry of its triple gables, planar expanses of brick, and large windows suggests an underlying modernism. The Arts and Crafts vocabulary also provided abundant opportunity for the clients to express their passion for authentic building materials. With interests extending well beyond the realm of wood, they became deeply involved in the selection and sourcing of hand-molded brick, the Himalayan slate of the roof, and the fieldstone of the gatehouses and guest cottage.

Inside the house, ivory-colored plaster walls and ceilings establish a neutral backdrop for imported woods, showcasing their warm colors and grain. Most of the architectural details, including segmental arches, barrel vaults, high baseboards, and deep cornices, are traditional in inspiration, but their pumped-up scale and clean lines create a contemporary effect. Nearly every room features at least two species of wood. The floors are composed of ten-inch-wide boards of French white oak, milled in the live-sawn method to expose more of their figured center grain than quarter-sawn boards. Casement windows and French doors manufactured by Asselin, a firm with decades of service to Versailles, the Louvre, and other European monuments, contribute to the rich mahogany-like glow of African moabi used throughout the house.

The oak paneling in the library, also by Asselin, was built to precise measurements in France, reassembled in Atlanta using traditional mortise, tenon, and pinned construction, and finished with a matte, translucent treatment that accentuates its character without

adding sheen. Using wood from the same stock, the husband produced the coffered ceiling in his molding plant. Although the paneling lends Old World refinement to the library, elements of its design, including the large, rectangular casings of the French doors and bookshelves, have more modern silhouettes.

To complement the couple's heirloom furniture, the primary entertaining rooms include traditional ceiling treatments that resemble run-in-place plaster moldings but are actually composed of wood. The Renaissance Revival pattern of the dining room ceiling, the interior molding of the cove ceiling in the living room, and the chevron surround of the stair hall

skylight were all custom-made by the husband's molding plant. In concert with the husband, who provided the book-matched burled walnut, and his wife, who collects Biedermeier furniture, we designed four new

ABOVE AND OPPOSITE: Seen from the top of the drive, the tall chimneys and vertical massing of this English Arts and Crafts–style house recall architect C. F. A. Voysey's country estates. Like many residences of that era, which were designed to accommodate chauffer-driven automobiles, the house has a secondary entrance facing a motor court. PRECEDING PAGES: The entry to the guest cottage behind the main house is a romantic reference to the English vernacular.

132

Biedermeier-style pieces—two china cabinets and two chests of drawers—to provide storage in the butler's pantry. The almost monastic simplicity of the plaster barrel vault provides an ideal setting for the furniture's strong lines and highly figured wood. In contrast, the nearby powder room is expressed almost entirely in wood, from its walls of striated Oriental wood to its ceiling of burled walnut. Unlike the usual feminine powder room, it is a dramatic, masculine space that calls to mind the interior of an Art Deco humidor.

With a palette of plants including Yorkstone and English roses, Southern camellias, and Korean boxwood, the landscaping is an outdoor extension of the house's global reinterpretation of traditional style. Roses growing in profusion over a rustic pergola and English vernacular guest cottage are charmingly pic-

turesque, while long borders of precisely pruned boxwood and the clean lines of the stone pool terrace lend a contemporary edge. Richard Anderson, the landscape architect, described the overall character of the grounds as "distilled"—a perfect way to express this house's new and harmonious blend of the past, present, and transcontinental.

ABOVE: The rose-covered pergola at the end of the pool terrace is both a charming focal point and a refuge from the sun.
OPPOSITE, TOP: The guest cottage, with walls of randomly sized, rough-hewn stone and a roof covered with dark wood shingles, opens onto the pool terrace. The crisp minimalism of the stone pool terrace and neatly trimmed boxwood hedges sets off more lush plantings of roses and flowering shrubs.
OPPOSITE, BOTTOM: A glass-enclosed porch overlooks an herb garden and boxwood hedge planted along one end of the pool terrace. From within the room, the oversized panes and thin steel muntins of the custom-made windows almost disappear, creating a sense of unity with the surrounding gardens.

ABOVE: Renaissance Revival–style ceiling moldings establish the formal character
of the dining room. Off-white cotton piqué seat covers and a pair of custom-designed
steel-and-soapstone serving tables add a modern Scandinavian note.
OPPOSITE: Over-scaled baseboards and doorways with robustly proportioned
cases have a strong, sculptural presence in the hall. Polished natural plaster
walls softly reflect light, evoking the pale luminosity of Scandinavian interiors.
OVERLEAF: The French oak paneling in the library was manufactured in
France by Asselin.

ABOVE: The powder room is finished in highly figured woods, with the strong lines of
Oriental wood, also known as Australian walnut, juxtaposed with a pattern of burled walnut.
OPPOSITE: In the master bedroom, the tray ceiling, detailed with concentric rectangles,
and the rectilinear wall paneling provide a hint of Art Deco style.

TROPICAL MERITAGE
Sea Island, Georgia

When a Chicago-based couple asked us to design their winter home in Sea Island, they originally envisioned a dwelling in the Mediterranean Revival style popularized by Addison Mizner, architect of The Cloister, the resort's original 1926 centerpiece. Before beginning sketches, however, I took them to tour a contemporaneous Sea Island cottage with classic Bermudan details designed by Philip Trammell Shutze, hoping to inspire them to consider an equally historic but less familiar style. We also looked at pictures of British colonial buildings in Bermuda, the Dutch colonial architecture of Cape Town and the West Indies, and the villas of Cuba and Brazil. Won over by the simple, almost modern floor plans and picturesque details shared by these various colonial styles, the clients agreed to design their second home in a hybrid aesthetic we dubbed "tropical meritage."

Dutch baroque gables, the zigzagging silhouette of step-tiled roofs, and hand-forged iron details that contrast with white stucco walls give the exterior of the residence an appearance that is simultaneously exotic and perfectly at home in the Georgia Sea Island setting. Instead of facing the street, the house addresses it sideways with a picturesque facade featuring paired gable ends, an exaggerated chimney, and an iron balcony. A gate with matching ironwork frames a path leading to the nearby beach. The primary facade is even more romantic, with a Dutch baroque–style entrance pavilion

flanked by asymmetrical wings, one based on a nineteenth-century Bermuda buttery and the other resembling a typical Bermuda cottage. At the rear of the house, an arcade reminiscent of colonial Cuban villas opens to a long, rectangular lawn and garden artfully designed by landscape architect John Howard, including a pool court and a 540-foot sweep of lawn bordered by palms, magnolias, camellias, and twenty live oaks transported to the site. This lush vista is visually anchored by a two-story garden pavilion that invokes the architecture of the house without repeating it.

It was a priority of the owners, who were seeking respite from Chicago's dark, cold winters, to have each room in the house interact closely with its natural surroundings, whether opening to an intimate garden, a private courtyard, or to the loggia. This fluid interaction between interior and exterior spaces—a universal aspect of tropical architecture, where cross-ventilation is a must—is particularly evident in the living room. This large, high-ceilinged room connects to the semi-sheltered sitting and dining areas on the loggia through four pairs of French doors that open to create a single pavilion-like space. Passages branching off from three corners of this central space lead to wings and ancillary rooms arranged around its periphery to maximize exposures.

In the conservatory-style breakfast room opening from the fourth corner of the room, floor-to-ceiling windows in every wall melt the boundaries between

interior and exterior space. Two glass-and-steel walls overlook garden terraces, another opens with a barn-style sliding glass door to the kitchen, and the fourth features wide bi-fold doors that unite the breakfast room and contiguous loggia. As one of the homeowners observed, the design of the house constantly shows you different ways to experience the relationship between "indoorness" and "outdoorness."

The owners told us that they wanted an open, modern plan, with a kitchen conveniently located for shared conversation and relaxed gatherings, without sacrificing well-defined entertaining spaces with a certain degree of formality. To accomplish this, we located the kitchen in an alcove-like space tucked beneath a low, elliptical ceiling that contrasts with the adjoining space's high, open-beamed, pitched ceiling.

The cooking and entertaining areas are further delineated by a tall island. By designing it to resemble an antique Spanish colonial table, we avoided introducing a clearly functional element into the primary living area—a common failing of open-plan kitchens. Despite this boundary, the kitchen complements and even enhances the adjoining room, with a white plaster stove hood that echoes the living room chimney breast and a wrought-iron pendant lamp that echoes the iron chandeliers and sconces.

Most architectural details in the house are expressed simply, with the exception of the highly decorative surrounds and transoms of the living room's French doors, which were inspired by project architect Greg Harrell's research of an early nineteenth-century Portuguese colonial villa in Brazil. Combining

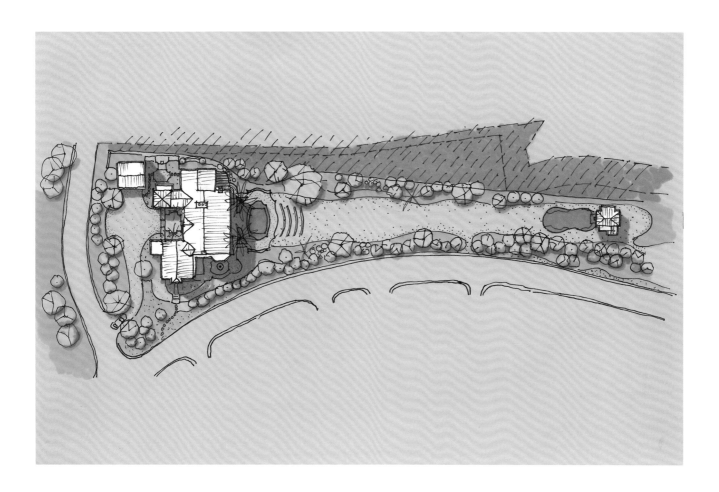

elements of the European baroque, including a hint of Chinese Chippendale, with robust colonial expression, their silhouettes, accented in turquoise, enliven the white walls and draw attention to the view beyond the doors. This element became a leitmotif used throughout the house, where architectural interest is also provided by surprising shifts in room shape and ceiling type. An octagonal antechamber with a raised bead-board ceiling serves as a transitional space between the entertaining rooms and master suite, which features a Bermuda-style tray ceiling. A barrel-vaulted ceiling adds a sense of mystery to the hallway leading to a square guest room, where a high pyramidal ceiling evokes an aura of island romance.

Whenever the opportunity arose, we incorporated handcrafted elements, including Spanish-style leaded glass, forged iron, and an antique door from an Argentine monastery, to contribute the tactile impression of age and authenticity. As the clients said after living in the house for a few months, "This house isn't just pretending to be something, it is something. Even though it's new, it feels as though it has old bones and an old soul."

PRECEDING PAGES: Elevated to afford views of the salt marsh, the beach, and the house, the gazebo terminates the vista from the house.
OPPOSITE: Marrying elements from several colonial island styles, including Bermudan and Dutch-West Indian, this house is a romantic improvisation. While the baroque curves of the pediment were inspired by continental and colonial Dutch architecture, the wing with its shed-roof porch resembles a typical West Indian cottage.

Custom-designed ironwork, including the balcony and gate on the street-
side facade, lantern mountings, sconces, and chandeliers provide graphic
contrast to wide expanses of bright white plaster. Although the overall design
of the house is simple, these details add touches of drama and romance.

PRECEDING PAGES: The large
central room parallels the loggia
and opens at one end to the
kitchen. When the French doors
are open, the room looks and
feels like an airy pavilion. Its high
ceiling draws warm air up and
natural light fills the space from
multiple sources.

RIGHT: In the loggia and
adjacent conservatory, matching
ceilings and lanterns imply that
the rooms were once part of a
larger, continuous porch.

ABOVE: In the master bathroom, Spanish-style leaded glass with hand-blown rondels adds decorative detail to a door that opens to a soaking tub with an Italian marble surround. Overlooking the lush island landscape through a large arched window, the bath chamber is a luxurious private oasis.
OPPOSITE: The exuberant Portuguese colonial–style door surround adds a strong decorative element in contrast to the spare architecture of the master bedroom.
OVERLEAF: Seen from the lawn, the rear facade, with its arcade, broad white roof, and triangular chimney caps, exemplifies the simplicity and visual drama of tropical colonial architecture.

FEDERAL FINESSE
Atlanta, Georgia

The land on which this house stands was originally part of a larger property occupied by one of Atlanta's Georgian-style Colonial Revival homes. Although the houses would be separated by an ample buffer, the seller of the land stipulated that the new residence be built in a style compatible to her own. Fortunately, both members of the couple acquiring the land hail from the antebellum Georgia town of Newnan and have a fine appreciation for neoclassical architecture, so this request was not cause for concern. During the yearlong design process that followed, the clients and I explored a variety of traditional American styles and floor plans. Their wish for wide, almost floor-to-ceiling windows eliminated early and mid-Georgian styles, and ultimately we arrived at a design inspired by the mid-Atlantic houses of the early Federal period. This fulfilled their vision of a formal, symmetrical, richly detailed house with qualities of elegance and warmth.

The new residence's brick facade is the epitome of restraint and order, belying the interior's more extravagant detail. From a distance, the classic five-bay, two-story main block appears sparingly embellished, decorated only with a single-story portico and an elliptical window in its pediment. On closer inspection, however, the portico turns out to be elaborately

conceived, with fluted columns and pilasters crowned by Tower of the Winds capitals. Below, the front door, surrounded by slender Ionic pilasters, sidelights, and a leaded-glass fanlight, hints at the lavish attention to detail in the entrance hall. That room is a showcase of early Federal aesthetics, with a full array of period elements including a highly articulated door surround and a dramatic screen of fluted columns that marks the transition to the stair hall.

In deference to the Federal period's aversion to fully paneled rooms, the entrance hall features recessed plaster panels inspired by those of the eighteenth-century British architect Robert Adam and embellished with egg-and-dart and pearl moldings. When interior designer Jackye Lanham and I discussed the decoration of the room, we agreed that the only period detail missing was a pair of Chippendale hall tables. Consulting Thomas Chippendale's 1784 pattern book, *The Gentleman and Cabinet-Maker's Director*, I designed a pair, fabricated with convincing historical finesse by Jim Nugent and finished by Howell Jones, who blunted the marble edges and even stained the surfaces lightly with ink to create a patina of long use.

The floor plan of the house follows the Federal period's inventive approach to room shape and relationship. Although the living and dining rooms are

arranged symmetrically on either side of the entrance hall, they do not open directly to each other. Instead, their doorways frame views that terminate in the entrance hall, establishing separation between the rooms and drawing attention to the hall's architectural details and furnishings. Enfilades trace transverse and longitudinal axes that meet in the center of the house, connecting the rooms and providing extended and intriguing sightlines. The two primary axes terminate in the demi-octagonal rooms favored by Federal architects. One is an intimate card room and the other an airy space with circle-head French doors that frame views of the rear garden. Located directly opposite the front door, this luminous room draws the eye through the house to connect with the surrounding landscape.

A variety of decorative details and contrasting materials add character to every room. The longest hall in the house is enhanced by a barrel-vaulted ceiling and double baseboard with a robust rope molding. In the small card room adjoining the living room, restrained moldings painted gray accentuate the brilliant French polish of doors with crotch-grain cherry veneer panels. Fluted pilasters flank the mantelpiece in the adjacent library, which is paneled with cherry wood finished to a rich, warm glow. Lighter colored northern pine resembling English deal imparts a more relaxed, country-house atmosphere to the family sitting room. In the dining room, a custom-designed marble-topped serving table with an original feather motif stands in an arched exedra. One night, well into a bottle of wine,

the interior designer and I came up with the idea of adding cornice boards above the dining room windows. These are painted in the style of Baltimore fancy chairs and depict the clients' three residences.

The clients' collections of English silver, Chinese porcelain, Native American artifacts, and Western paintings and sculpture—including bronze figures by sculptor Frederic Remington—complete the decoration of each room. Although such a combination might seem unlikely at first, it is true to the eclecticism that was a hallmark of Federal taste. Thomas Jefferson's collection at Monticello is a notable example. Despite its grace, elegance, and delicacy, the Federal aesthetic is also one of America's most adventurous styles. Fully embodying all these characteristics, this house expresses both its form and its essence in a setting that is as personal as it is true to period style.

OPPOSITE AND PRECEDING PAGES: This Federal-style residence has a dignified, symmetrical five-bay facade of handmade brick with random glazed headers interspersed. The portico features the Tower of the Winds capitals that came into vogue after the 1750s publication of *Antiquities of Athens* by James Stuart and Nicholas Revett.
ABOVE: The screen of columns and pilasters dividing the entrance hall from the central stair hall also incorporates Tower of the Winds capitals. Inspired by Baltimore's historic Homewood house (c. 1800), the entrance hall floor is white marble with black cabochons.

PRECEDING PAGES: Neoclassical motifs including a pediment over blind entablature, split Ionic capitals, Doric pilasters, and varied patterns of marble parquet distinguish the entrances to important rooms. RIGHT: An arched exedra accommodating a custom-designed serving table adds a focal point to the wall between the dining room and the entrance hall. Door cases are embellished with fluted friezes and gilded rosettes and capped with projecting classical cornices. Handsome by day, walls covered in red silk, black cornice boards inspired by Baltimore fancy chairs, and beige wainscoting are even more beautiful by candlelight.

ABOVE: Four nearly floor-to-ceiling windows bring natural light into
a library paneled in cherry wood with a rich amber finish that accentuates
its grain. This intimate room offers a handsome setting for collections
of Western art, English furniture, and Chinese exportware.
OPPOSITE: In the demi-octagonal card room, crotch-grain cherry-wood panels
add drama to French-polished mahogany doors. This intimate room connects
the living room and library, making its built-in bar convenient to both.

ABOVE: The central stair hall is naturally illuminated from both sides and from above by a skylight. Positioned directly beneath the chandelier, a black cabochon marks the point where the house's two primary axes intersect.
OPPOSITE, FROM TOP LEFT: Tower of the Winds capitals on the screen opening to the stair hall; a leaded glass transom over the front door; neoclassical motifs include a decorative anthemia relief and egg-and-dart moldings.
OVERLEAF: French doors in the bay of the rear facade open onto the garden.

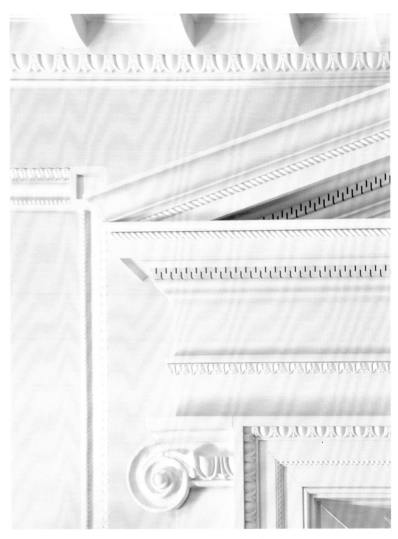

SOUTHERN GOTHIC COTTAGE

Atlanta, Georgia

Although this house is small, conforming to the footprint of the 1934 cottage that previously occupied the site, it is generous in style and personality. The clients had hoped to renovate the older dwelling, but after discovering irreversible termite and water damage, they asked me to design a new house that complemented the architecture of the surrounding neighborhood. Although the new house could not be much larger than the original, the clients wanted a good number of rooms, including two guest suites for visiting children and grandchildren, formal living and dining rooms, an informal family room, a home office, and a library. Our goal became the creation of a cottage-style dwelling that incorporated the required rooms without sacrificing Southern qualities of graciousness, comfort, and charm.

This is the third house I've designed in collaboration with this couple and their interior designer, Jackye Lanham. One of the many reasons I enjoy working with them is that they have open minds when it comes to design and are willing to entertain unexpected ideas. As a result, the house is filled with delightful quirks and surprises that make it as engaging as the neighboring cottages and bungalows.

Like the original residence, the new house faces the quiet street with a screened porch deep enough to serve as an outdoor sitting room in pleasant weather. Unlike its predecessor, however, the house is entered from the side, through a gate leading to a brick courtyard shaded by a specimen mountain laurel and saucer magnolias. Every detail of the exterior, from the portico's carpenter-style brackets and outriggers to its many gables and windows of varied shapes and sizes, contributes to its cottage appeal.

In designing the interior, I discarded all preconceived notions about the archetypal Southern house. Because every inch counted, the rooms had to flow directly from one to the next and some had to serve two functions. An enfilade running the full length of the house provides an uninterrupted vista. Terminating at one end with a pair of French doors that open to the porch and at the other with a pivoting oval window, this enfilade conveys a feeling of grace and spaciousness. It also provides easy access to all the rooms in the house, including those on the second floor.

In keeping with the cottage flavor, we decided on interior walls of bead board. Walls and ceilings of wide poplar board painted a soft shade of ivory provide the perfect backdrop for more ornamental and fanciful details. While maintaining the overall simplicity of the design, we seized every opportunity to add interest and charm to even the smallest room.

Instead of downplaying the staircase that shares space in the dining room, I accentuated it with a demilune interior window and a shapely banister painted

dark brown to contrast with the walls. To give equal weight to the dining area, I added a box beam, from which the interior designer hung a crystal chandelier to visually anchor the table beneath.

To mitigate the potentially awkward shape of the narrow living room, I added a quirky yet handsome mantelpiece that's a bit over-scaled for the space. For the very tall spaces on either side of the mantel, I designed a pair of built-in cabinets with trefoil Gothic arches supported by clustered columns. These inspired other Gothic-style details, including the arched mullions of the living room French doors and a wall of bookcases in the family sitting room decorated with Gothic arches and colonnettes. In contrast, the master bedroom is pure Southern vernacular in style. While two square windows with plain muntins and barn-style shutters add an almost rustic note, simple pilasters flanking a wide bay of casement windows recall the

pared-down neoclassical detail often found in rural Southern houses.

Outside, a garden was created in collaboration with the clients and landscape architect Richard Anderson. The property ends just beyond the handkerchief-sized lawn, but a large arched door set within its Tennessee fieldstone retaining wall suggests that the garden continues on its other side. A bit like an English folly, this unexpected feature adds the final dose of romance to a twenty-first-century cottage that might easily have been built a hundred years ago.

ABOVE: This new cottage, built to conform to the small, narrow footprint of the 1934 house that stood there before, is a perfect complement to the neighboring bungalows.
OPPOSITE: Glazed pocket doors between the library and living room create a sense of spaciousness by sharing light and views.
PRECEDING PAGES: In the living room the large fireplace nearly fills one of the short walls. The narrow spaces on either side suggested Gothic forms, which became a motif in the house.

Serving as dining area, stair hall, and passageway, the dining room was carefully designed to accommodate all functions. Locating the staircase on one wall and arranging the table off center allows circulation, while the box beam on the ceiling anchors the table in the space.

Gothic motifs reappear in the family room, where a wall of built-in bookcases holds collections of books, antiques, glass, brass, china and boxes, and in the bar, where the Gothic arch adds an impression of height to the diminutive space.

HEIRLOOM HOUSE
Atlanta, Georgia

This project began with a call from a client who wanted me to improve the flow of her entrance hall, which tended to bottleneck during parties. After touring the house with her and offering a few suggestions about reconfiguring the hall, I overheard her husband say, "Did you tell Norman that you never liked the outside of the house?" When I stepped into the yard to take a better look and find out what the client had in mind, she said that if it were possible to start from scratch, she'd build a residence in the style of a farmhouse. Looking at the rather plain-vanilla 1980s brick facade, it was hard to imagine achieving such a complete change of character, but I told her we could certainly add a porch and charm things up a bit. I don't think any of us realized how completely transformed the house would be at the end of two years.

Soon after we began working together, the client inherited a sizeable collection of antique furniture, folk art, and decorative objects from her parents, and she asked me to help integrate them into the house. Having worked previously with her mother and father, I was already familiar with many of these objects. Ultimately, the collection defined the project, which became about rethinking, reframing, and reinterpreting a house and heirlooms, treating them not as inanimate objects, but as living things that would continue to be enjoyed for years to come.

The first changes we made were to the front of the house, where we added a porch with gracious Southern appeal. Although it is beautifully situated with a very private front lawn and acres of woodlands behind, the house offered little opportunity for appreciating the setting. The new front porch, enclosed on two sides with lattice and raised just a short step above the lawn, provides a pleasant place to sit and enjoy the surroundings. With benches built into its walls, lamps for reading, and old-fashioned ceiling fans, it is a true outdoor living room and is used almost daily.

The house originally had a rear deck, but the owners rarely used it. We replaced it with a long sunroom with floor-to-ceiling windows, creating an everyday sitting and dining area that nestles into the forest's canopy like a tree house. When we remodeled the adjacent kitchen, we removed a wall, uniting it in an open plan with the new dining area and giving it an expansive view of the woods as well.

The remodeling also included the addition of a large office for the husband on the lower floor, complete with a small golf practice area, and a charming office for his wife, located beneath the eaves of the new third floor. Moving the master bedroom from the front of the house to the rear transformed it into a private woodland retreat, while also creating space for an ultra-feminine dressing room with mirrored cabinets,

LEFT AND PRECEDING PAGES:
A generously proportioned
front porch and three dormer
windows add character to this
1980s brick house. Combined
with a pair of existing brick
chimneys and a new jerkinhead
roof, these elements bring
the house closer to the ideal of
an early American farmhouse.
The porch was inspired by
Charleston houses, using
traditional Doric pillars and
pilasters and checkerboard
marble tiles, with lattice walls
and built-in benches adding
contemporary appeal.

181

Reconfiguring the staircase created wall space to accommodate an inherited collection of twentieth-century American folk art. Multiple light sources, including a lantern, a chandelier, a bay of second-story windows, and a dormer window provide even lighting in this dramatic vertical gallery.

floor-to-ceiling shoe shelves, a central organizing table, and a window seat overlooking the lawn. Years earlier I had designed a lavish dressing room for the client's mother that was the talk of Atlanta, and I wanted my client to have one that was equally beautiful. In what has become a rarity for men, a handsome dressing room on the other side of the bedroom provides equal closet space for her husband.

Working with interior designer Susan Bozeman, we re-envisioned each room with the heirlooms as our guide. We began with the stair hall, transforming it into a vertical gallery for early American folk paintings. In the dining room, more than a dozen eighteenth- and nineteenth-century European tea-warmers, called

veilleuses, are arrayed on a Regency-style parcel gilt cabinet-on-stand I designed. More are displayed on similar Regency-style brackets arranged in groupings on the velvet-covered walls.

In the living room, additional warmth, charm, and display space are provided by new Colonial Revival–style cabinetry, including a wall-width breakfront with shelves for books and a pair of cabinets with arched fronts and beadboard backing. The new paneling also includes a rectangular reveal above the mantel designed to accommodate a large, primitive American portrait. To make the space more sympathetic to a collection of small-scale New England antiques, we reduced its apparent height with the addition of a wide, central sum-

mer beam and a pair of diminutive iron chandeliers suspended on either side. Arranging four comfortable upholstered chairs among the more delicate wood pieces, Bozeman succeeded in disarming the room's formality, transforming it into an inviting fireside gathering place.

In the adjoining family room, we replaced the original bland blond paneling with character-grade oak, oxidized to achieve a soft, weathered patina that complements the faded tones of a large antique needlework portrait of George Washington. Exposed beams, an iron chandelier, and hand-forged sconces give the room an early American atmosphere inspired in part by a hand-sewn flag that hangs above the sofa. Instead of treating these rare textiles as if they belonged behind

glass in a museum, we integrated them into a room where they're enjoyed every day. When the clients said, "We love these things, we plan to use them, and we don't want to feel like we are tiptoeing around them," we took them at their word.

The front door is faux-finished in two different styles. On the interior is the expressive faux-graining popular in nineteenth-century America and an antique English carpenter lock; outside, a decorative finish resembling weathered paint give the door the texture and appearance of age.
OVERLEAF: The walls of the dining room are upholstered in a rich, neutral beige to complement a collection of highly decorative eighteenth- and nineteenth-century tea warmers, known in France as *veilleuses*.

In the living room, new Colonial Revival–style paneled cabinetry provides display space
and adds architectural interest. The warm red of the beadboard backing accentuates
the shapes and patterns of antique English china and salt-glaze cream ware. A summer
beam reduces the apparent height of the ceiling, improving the proportions of the
room and enhancing the setting for the collection of small-scale New England antiques.

Replacing a deck with a large sunroom not only opened the rear of the house to the surrounding woods, but also added a bright sitting area and a casual dining space next to the kitchen. The room is furnished with informal antiques, including an English bamboo sofa, an iron floor lamp, and a Welsh dresser containing old serving platters. OVERLEAF: The family room is paneled in character-grade oak with checks, splits, and worm holes and oxidized for a dry, gray finish that complements the early nineteenth-century flag and the needlework portrait of George Washington.

ABOVE: Replacing the original gable with a steep jerkinhead roof made it possible to accommodate a cove ceiling in the master bedroom, adding elegance and increasing height. Even so, the four-poster bed seemed tall for the space, so we interrupted the cornice above where it would stand. Moved from the front of the house to the back, the bedroom now overlooks the protected woodlands through windows framed by decorative wooden valances.
OPPOSITE: With a flat ceiling painted to resemble a garden-party tent, cabinets with mirrored doors, a silver-leaf chandelier, and window seats, the dressing room combines utility with whimsy and elegance. Gilded trim and crystal knobs dress up a "pleather"-topped custom chest that serves both as a packing table and storage for accessories.

SKY CASTLE

Cashiers, North Carolina

I've always thought that the small mountainside castles in the Dordogne region of France are among the most romantic houses in the world. When I was asked to design a stone house on a steep mountainside in western North Carolina, these ancient châteaux, called *gentilhommières*, were the first thing that came to mind. In a dramatic natural site like this, whatever is built needs to look as if it has grown right up out of the earth. In Dordogne, many of the houses have foundations cut directly into the limestone on which they stand. They literally can't be separated from the ground or the surrounding landscape—and that's what I thought should happen here.

There was already a small house on the property, which we had designed for the clients several years earlier. Like many of the region's early dwellings, it nestles into the trees for protection, peeping over the edge of the mountain without leaving cover of the woods. With exterior walls clad in chestnut bark—one of the area's distinctive vernacular building materials—the cottage looks and feels very much as if it is part of the forest. The new house is much more exposed. Constructed primarily of heavy, rough-hewn fieldstone, the house sits directly on the earth. A commanding square tower with a picturesque cap of a roof points up toward the clouds, adding a dose of charm to the rugged facade.

When you walk through the massive front door into this tower, it is easy to forget that you are still in North Carolina, or even in the modern age. A staircase fashioned with mortise-and-tenon construction from reclaimed chestnut boards speckled with checks and splits is illuminated by shafts of light that float down from windows set into substantial stone walls. The balusters, while expressed in country-carpenter style, have an elegant baroque silhouette that suggests that they were added to the "original" staircase a few centuries after its construction. Such architectural narratives are often found in Dordogne stone houses, many of which were built as fortified castles during the Hundred Years' War and later transformed into mountain retreats. Rugged and somewhat stern on the outside, they are surprisingly charming and inviting within.

The largest room in the house is the twenty-two-foot long living room, which has a ceiling of reclaimed barn wood and hand-adzed pine beams salvaged from a church in Georgia. The weathered surface of the pine, combined with the rich grain of antique French oak floorboards, warms the room with an underlying glow. Variations in texture and color and slightly rounded corners give the hand-troweled plaster walls an antique appearance, enhanced by a mantelpiece made from three huge slabs of local stone. A large ganged window pierces the north-facing wall of the living room, framing a far-reaching vista of mountains and sky. Protected by the deep overhang of a pent roof, the window brings in diffused light that accentuates the texture of the natural materials.

Each room in the house is sited to take advantage of varying light effects throughout the day. Located on

the northwestern corner, the master bedroom is softly illuminated in the morning and radiant in the afternoon. A low-pitched ceiling that combines natural wood crossbeams with boards painted a shade of white reflects the light, creating an atmosphere of airy brightness. East-facing windows flood the kitchen on the other end of the house with morning light that plays on the varied-colored antique brick of a huge wall oven. Inspired by one in a centuries-old kitchen in a French farmhouse, this replica includes a raised hearth with a working fireplace surrounded by niches that originally would have functioned as ovens for cooking food at different temperatures. With the refrigerator hidden from sight in an adjoining pantry and upper cabinets designed to resemble antique cupboards, the stainless steel range is the room's only obvious concession to modernity.

While the materials and craftsmanship of the facade and interior spaces are intended to transport you to ancient France, the back porch is true to its North Carolina setting. Constructed in pure Blue Ridge Mountain vernacular style, the porch is built in the timber-frame manner, with posts and rails made from locust trees felled on the property, and the rear walls are covered with chestnut-bark shingles. Unlike the stone facade of the house, which hugs the ground, the rear porch soars above the steep grade on tall timber poles. The front of the house promises shelter and protection from the elements, but the rear reaches out to the natural setting with an open-air living and dining room that hangs over the mountain's edge. Balanced between earth and sky, the house bridges two worlds, offering a rustically romantic setting from which to enjoy the timeless beauty of nature.

Inspired by the medieval châteaux of the Dordogne, the house hugs the ground with heavy stone walls and a broad, shingled roof that sweeps low in areas. Vines creeping over its fieldstone walls and the naturally weathered appearance of chestnut-bark and wood-shake shingles lend a sense of age and permanence.

ABOVE: Unlike the stone entrance facade, the rear of the main house is designed in the same Blue Ridge Mountain vernacular style as the nearby guest cottage. Both are clad in chestnut-bark shingles.
OPPOSITE: Built literally out of the surrounding forest, the guest cottage looks and feels like a tree house. The small front porch offers a pleasant vantage point from which to view the rock garden. The large back porch provides both an open-air sitting and dining area and a place to nap beneath a timber-frame roof.

In the stone stair tower, thick wood treads echo with the sound of footsteps, and light filters down through windows that decrease in size as they ascend. Based on an eighteenth-century rural European precedent, the balusters are sophisticated in concept but vernacular in execution. At the top, a massive iron chandelier hangs from a pyramidal ceiling sheathed in reclaimed wormy chestnut.

OVERLEAF: In keeping with the simplicity of medieval architecture in the Dordogne, the interior has no baseboards, cornices, or other decorative trim. In the living room, the hand-adzed pine ceiling, roughly plastered walls, and the massive stone fireplace complement furniture and architectural elements that the clients acquired in France.

A short hall separates the living room from the master bedroom suite, offering privacy
and providing a bright space for a small writing desk. Opposite the desk, a pair of rustic
armoire doors from France conceals storage for modern stereo equipment.

ABOVE: Inspired by examples in French and Italian farmhouses, the master bedroom
ceiling combines rugged beams with painted boards that lighten their impression.
OPPOSITE: With handsome oak floors and a mountain view, the master bathroom feels like
a small bedroom retrofitted into a bathroom in the early days of modern plumbing.

The centerpiece of the kitchen is a replica of an eighteenth-century French kitchen fireplace with pocket wall ovens. Hand-trowelled plaster walls, rough-hewn beams, salvaged pine board, and an iron chandelier create a rustic atmosphere, enhanced by the farm table in the middle of the room. Cabinetry is unobtrusive, with wall cabinets designed to resemble antique cupboards. OVERLEAF: Projecting over the steep slope, the back porch commands expansive mountain views. In keeping with the regional vernacular, the posts and railings are locust wood, prized by local carpenters for their hard wood, straight trunks, and durability. The outdoor fireplace is constructed in the local stacked-stone.

CLASSICAL FAMILY HOUSE
Atlanta, Georgia

There is a tendency to think of classical architecture as something suited more to an adult, formal way of life rather than relaxed, intergenerational family living. In reality, the classically inspired house has always been intended for both. During the Italian Renaissance, Andrea Palladio and his contemporaries began adapting classical prototypes to residential architecture, bringing the disciplines of balance and order and Greco-Roman forms and detail to the Italian farmhouse and giving rise to the classic Italian villa. But despite its elevated aesthetics, the villa was still a home in which children were raised and farms were managed. Balancing beauty with practicality and comfort, the villa became a major source of inspiration for domestic architecture on both sides of the Atlantic from the seventeenth through the mid-nineteenth century. When a couple with three young children commissioned us to design an Italian-style house combining classical architecture with a livable plan, we proposed a design based on this enduring precedent.

The site chosen by the clients was perfect—a mini-Monticello atop a small hill. By grading and filling the upper portion of the site, we created a plateau long enough to accommodate the house and extensive grounds including a pool, a recreational lawn, and formal gardens. Like the villas that inspired it, the house rests directly on the earth, giving the facade a much more approachable, friendly demeanor than if it had been raised on a masonry plinth. The symmetry of the central block and flanking wings is precise, and the details, including a pediment, engaged portico, and Doric colonnades, are classically correct. But other than the use of dressed limestone for the most refined elements, the facade is composed of stucco over masonry, an informal material recalling rural Italian houses built of fieldstone or brick finished with stucco. Although the sienna-colored stucco is scored on the corners of the main block to resemble quoins, the remainder is intentionally rustic, with variations in tone and a slightly rough, uneven texture.

Like the facade, the entrance hall is elegant but not intimidating. As in all but the most ornate Italian villas, it has large expanses of undecorated wall with only a few openings for windows and doors. An impressive two-story spiral stair crowned by a domed rotunda fulfilled the clients' request for a circular stair like those of the great seventeenth- and eighteenth-century European houses. To balance its impact, the other architectural elements in the hall are generous in scale and articulation. Like the Mannerist architects

who exaggerated classical forms for decorative effect, we designed a highly embellished classical surround for the living room entrance. The doorway is extremely tall, leading the eye upward with a projecting pediment that extends all the way to the cornice. These details elevate the refinement of the entrance hall, but a floor paved with random rectangular stone cut from the top layer of Europe's ancient Roman roads grounds the space, providing a rugged and durable surface for daily traffic by children.

In addition to providing access to the formal living room and second-floor bedrooms, the stair hall also serves as an axis connecting the front entrance with the

PRECEDING PAGES: Like the Renaissance-era Italian country villas that inspired it, this house combines rigorous symmetry and classical motifs with earthy materials and an approachable demeanor.
ABOVE, LEFT: With high ceilings, large expanses of wall, and minimal trim, the entrance hall is restrained. Against this backdrop, an exaggerated door surround featuring a mannerist amalgam of classical forms is a powerful statement.
ABOVE, RIGHT: Opposite the front door, another highly decorated casement opens from the entrance hall to a gallery flanked by a kitchen and breakfast room and the family living room.
OPPOSITE: Within the uncluttered decoration and warm tones of the entrance hall, the circular stair has a strong, masculine presence.

the back of the property are expansive, they are also private, surrounded by woods and enclosed on one side by a recreational wing that accommodates a pool house and gymnasium.

Designed in collaboration with landscape architects Hugh and Mary Palmer Dargan, the grounds and gardens adhere to the axial principles of Italian Renaissance landscape design. With straight borders of neatly pruned boxwoods, shaded gravel paths, and a long rectangle of lawn, the rear property has the cool, calming aspect of a country Italian pleasure garden. The recreational wing is reminiscent of an antique *limonaia*—an orangerie-like greenhouse for lemons. The Dargans balanced the pool house and adjacent terrace with a large shade garden on the opposite side of the lawn featuring a koi pond with a Renaissance-style stone surround. A pair of antique iron gates with massive, rusticated limestone piers stands at the bottom of the garden on axis with the house. Relics from a French château, the gates are always left ajar, issuing an invitation to climb the wide steps to a limestone terrace surrounded by roses and natural woodland. Although the terrace reinforces the garden's principles of symmetry and order, its message is one of romance—the perfect ending for a house that is a romantic reverie about another time and place.

family's living areas at the rear of the house. Opposite the front door, an arched casement that is only slightly less ornamental than the living room entrance leads to a hall terminating in French doors that open to a terrace. The kitchen and a sunken family sitting room flank the hall in an almost modern, open-plan arrangement that allowed the owners to keep an eye on their children, whether they were indoors or out in the yard. As is often the case in southern European houses, there is an easy flow between interior and exterior spaces that takes full advantage of a temperate climate with an extended blooming season. The rear facade features two short wings that turn the terrace into an intimate courtyard and provide views and multiple exposures to the rooms within. While the gardens and lawns extending toward

ABOVE: Although the engaged portico with a robust broken segmental pediment makes an impressive statement, the entrance is raised just a few steps above ground. The iron lanterns were among the architectural elements acquired in Europe for the house. OPPOSITE: A pair of antique French gates mounted between rusticated limestone pillars marks the transition from the formal architecture of the house and its gardens to the surrounding woods. OVERLEAF: Contrasting with the reserve of the front of the house, the rear-facing rooms project and recede. With French doors that open directly to the stone terrace and long, low ground-floor windows, the north-facing rooms are closely integrated with outdoor living areas.

SOUTHERN CLASSIC
Atlanta, Georgia

You can take the Southerner out of the South, but you can't take the South out of a Southerner. That is the lesson of this house, owned by a couple who spent years in Indianapolis and France before returning to Georgia. Although the husband's business had taken them far afield, his wife continued to dream of living in a classic Southern house in Atlanta. Even before they returned, a friend found what she thought was their ideal home—a 1952 Colonial Revival residence designed by Clem Ford, one of Atlanta's leading architects at the time. Built in the Greek Revival style, the house had many elements the couple desired, including a gracious center hall plan with well-proportioned entertaining rooms, but it was also dated and lacking in distinctive detail. Nonetheless, the couple recognized that the house had good bones and great potential, and chose it as their new home.

The reworking of the house was substantial. It included adding an entire new back to the house and a substantial bedroom wing, remodeling the basement and wine cellar, and constructing a pool pavilion in a rear garden redesigned by landscape architect Richard Anderson. We brightened the red brick exterior of the house by painting it a creamy shade of white, accentuating the beauty of its classical forms. We then replaced a pair of narrow sidelights with better proportioned ones and added an over-scaled front door embellished with shallow turkey-breast panels on the outside and crotch-grain mahogany within. The entrance hall's ceiling height was too low to accommodate the elliptical transom the transformation called for, but by removing the original over-door balcony, we created enough space to install a blind transom that instantly made the house look taller and more refined.

Having spent a great deal of time in Charleston, the owners had developed an appreciation for the beautiful interior moldings of Federal and Greek Revival dwellings. Unfortunately, the nine-foot ceilings in their own house were too low for a generously scaled cornice, so we designed one that is shorter than usual but quite intricate, making it appear taller than it actually is and also increasing the apparent height of the ceiling. A lower-than-usual paneled wainscot in the dining room, combined with Zuber scenic wallpaper, produces a similar effect.

A spacious center hall with a tempting vista at its end—usually a beautiful stair—is an iconic element of a classic Southern house, but the proportions of the entrance hall of this house were constrained and the staircase was anticlimactic. To give the hall greater sophistication, we embellished it with new decorative

details, including a Fortuny wall covering and a marble floor with a compass-shaped medallion that points toward the stair hall. The pièce de résistance is the new stair—an architectural confection visible the moment the front door opens. Although the dimensions were tight, we took cues from the French—who are masters of stair articulation—in designing a graceful stair that seems to dance its way up to the floor above. Crowned by a new leaded glass skylight, the striking stair hall is bathed in natural light throughout the day and illuminated by a crystal chandelier at night.

While these changes increased the elegance of the entertaining rooms, alterations across the back of the house were designed to accommodate casual daily living and visits from an extended family including six grandchildren. We reconfigured the large kitchen to create a sitting area with a fireplace and a combined prep-kitchen and pantry where clutter can be confined. More recently, we enclosed a screened porch adjacent to the kitchen with French doors, providing even more space for family gatherings. On the other end of the house, a new wing accommodates a master suite with decorative details reminiscent of old Louisiana houses and a pine-paneled study inspired by the offices of South Carolina plantations. Room finishes, from the study's paneling to the living room's pale blue-green walls, were chosen to complement the couple's extensive collection of Southern art and antiques. In the wide new hall added across the back of the house, soft white walls accentuate colorful early twentieth-century paintings, antique wood furniture, and a pair of André Arbus–inspired cabinets designed for the space.

Once very contained, the rear of the house now has a bright, open feel and expansive views of the gardens, including a pavilion that serves as a focal point at the far end of the pool terrace. Positioned between the pool and the heretofore underappreciated rear portion of the property, the pavilion offers a view of woodlands where the owners intend to reconstruct a log cabin built by Cherokee Indians and owned by their Georgia ancestors. When the cabin is in place, yet another layer of history will be added to this house, which, like the best of old Southern dwellings, honors the past and promises to remain in the memories of future generations.

ABOVE AND PRECEDING PAGES: The new stair is designed in the French manner, with a very tall upward sweep accentuated by a sinuous mahogany rail. Trompe l'oeil details and a leaded glass skylight add elegance to the space.
OPPOSITE: The house has archetypal Southern features, including a stately Ionic portico and center hall plan. The original red brick is now painted white to accentuate its classical forms and brighten its north-facing facade.

ABOVE: Raising the height of the door surround to within inches of the cornice increases the apparent verticality of the living room entrance. The new door casing features a corkscrew motif inspired by a Charleston precedent.
OPPOSITE: A tricolor marble floor medallion, Fortuny wall coverings, and an ormolu chandelier add elegance to the entance hall.

PRECEDING PAGES, LEFT:
Interior details include
handsome volutes
terminating the stair rails
and the Greek key motif
applied throughout.
PRECEDING PAGES, RIGHT:
Hand-blocked wallpaper
from Zuber's *Les Jardins
Francais* pattern, first
produced in 1822, is installed
in the dining room.
RIGHT: A series of garden
rooms behind the house
includes a Pennsylvania
bluestone terrace and a
formal boxwood garden with
an antique Italian wellhead in
its center. The new master
bedroom wing extends from
the main block to wrap one
side of the terrace.

MEDITERRANEAN ROMANCE
Palm Beach, Florida

Florida's early Mediterranean Revival houses are among the most romantic buildings ever constructed on American soil. The commission we received to design a Palm Beach waterfront villa in this style provided a welcome opportunity to revisit the architecture of Addison Mizner and his contemporaries, as well as the Italian, Spanish, and Spanish colonial architecture that inspired them. It also offered an irresistible invitation to surrender to unbridled creativity. Although its forms are rooted in history, the spirit of the Mediterranean Revival is one of invention—as the great villas of Palm Beach, Coral Gables, and Coconut Grove eloquently attest.

Project architect William Litchfield describes this villa as a house that unveils itself slowly. Suspense builds as the drive tunnels through a jungle-like allée of Alexander palms before arriving at a forecourt bordered by an arcade and a charming terra-cotta tile-roofed garage. Constructed of hand-carved coquina columns, stuccoed arches, and antique barrel tiles, the arcade offers glimpses of a large courtyard with a fifteenth-century marble fountain in its center. Entering the arcade, a deliberately exaggerated Mannerist door surround comes into view on the far side of the courtyard. Although it is tempting to cross the courtyard and enter between its massive banded engaged columns, the arcade's brick walkway travels laterally, terminating on one end at the entrance to a separate guest suite and on the other, in a shadowy porch that shelters the iron-studded and paneled cypress front door.

Rather than opening into an entrance hall with solid walls, the door leads to another arcade, this one with a row of French doors overlooking the courtyard and a screen of Andalusian-style coquina columns framing views of the dining room. Blurring the boundaries between interior and exterior space, this arcade brings filtered light, the scent of flowers, and the sounds of the splashing fountain into the space, even when the French doors are shut. The fragrance of the heavy oak ceiling beams, like the texture of the arcade's hand-carved columns, creates an immediate impression of antiquity, or what one of the owners refers to as "another layer of soul."

This romantic entrance hall traces an axis from the front door of the house to the living room and beyond, continuing through French doors to terminate in a generously proportioned loggia overlooking a lake. The H-shaped house has four wings branching off from the long central living room. Although this plan offers opportunities for strong axes, it provides just as many off-axial moments that create a sense of intrigue. For example, while the living room is perfectly symmetrical, with windows and doors that open directly across from one another to the courtyard and the loggia, it can be entered only from the corners and must be traversed, sometimes diagonally, to the rooms on either side. This arrangement provides the primary rooms two, and often three, exposures, and creates a sequence of spaces that relate as much or more to the landscape as to each other. Nearly every room opens to the central cloister, a side

courtyard, or the loggia, and all have beautiful views of the natural setting and sumptuous gardens designed by Cuban-born Jorge Sanchez, principal of the landscape architecture firm Sanchez & Maddox.

Taking cues from Spanish, Italian, Moroccan, and early Palm Beach houses, the interior is lavishly embellished with period details, including the Moorish star of the cypress-paneled ceiling in the dining room and the Spanish-style corbels and rope motif moldings of the living room. Traveling to Europe, New Mexico, and New Orleans with the clients and their interior designer, Carolyn Malone, we collected antique hardware, light fixtures, and furnishings for the house-in-progress. As excited as we were with our discoveries, we forced ourselves to be disciplined in our final choices, as the Mediterranean Revival style, though highly ornamented, is also characterized by a restraint that sometimes crosses into austerity.

Builder Randy Webb employed a group of craftsmen versed in Old World building arts, including stone carvers, master carpenters, and plasterers. Working with authentic materials like pigmented Venetian plaster and antique French limestone, they created interior finishes indistinguishable from the antique ones that inspired them. One of the most challenging of these was the neoclassical trelliswork of the gazebo-like room at the rear of the house, which was inspired not by Mediterranean architecture, but by a room designed by Ogden Codman and Edith Wharton in Newport, Rhode Island. An unexpected departure from the rest of the house, it stands as a testament to the broad eclecticism that fueled the imagination and creativity of late nineteenth-century American architects. When you discover this little folly of a room at the back of the house, surrounded on three sides by tropical vistas, you are reminded that the true secret of romance is the element of surprise.

OPPOSITE AND PRECEDING PAGES: This residence has a romantic entrance sequence that leads through an arcade and along a courtyard. Pebble mosaics, a marble medallion, and a fifteenth-century Moroccan fountain create a serene and sensuous atmosphere. An exaggerated Mannerist-style door surround with banded engaged columns in dressed limestone was salvaged from a Palm Beach mansion.

ABOVE: The arcade is composed of hand-carved coquina columns below a barrel
roof of French terra-cotta tiles supported by rustic cypress beams.
OPPOSITE, FROM TOP LEFT: The custom-made cypress front door designed in the
Spanish colonial style; the bold profile of the Mannerist door surround; a niche for
a nineteenth-century bust; intricate pebble mosaic in the courtyard.

In the dining room, a large Spanish trestle table is surrounded by high-backed carved chairs. Reflected light from the courtyard flows in through the arcade. Paneled in the shape of an eight-pointed star, the ceiling is made of pecky cypress, a popular material with Florida's Mediterranean Revival architects. Its strong grain, rich tone, and rugged texture provide a rustic counterpoint to the European chandelier. OVERLEAF: The living room is the full width of the house, with French doors opening to the courtyard on one side and to the loggia on the other. Instead of formal circulation, the plan of the house provides arcades, open-sided galleries, and wide spaces like the living room and loggia that double as passageways.

ABOVE: A Spanish Colonial–style foliate window surrounded by a collection of decorative plates is the focal point of the office.
OPPOSITE: Inspired by a room in Newport, Rhode Island, by Ogden Codman and Edith Wharton, the breakfast room combines neoclassical details with more whimsical lattice.

The cool gray-green color and stone-like texture of the walls of the master bedroom are a soothing contrast to the bright tropical views framed by the windows. Plaster carved to look like eighteenth-century paneling complements the rococo curves of the giltwood headboard.

246

ABOVE: Antique decorative objects, including the pendant lamp in the guest bath and the baroque wall fountain used as a lavatory in the powder bath, contribute Old World character to even the smallest rooms.

OPPOSITE: The loggia is a transitional space between the interior and the boxwood garden. A comfortable outdoor sitting room, it also serves as a sheltered passageway between the breakfast room and master bedroom wing.

OVERLEAF: The rear facade evokes a classical Italian villa. An Italianate balustrade marks the boundary between the formal garden and the lake shore.

PROJECT CREDITS

VILLA VECCHIA

Project Manager: Jim McConnell
Builder: Mickey Watkins
Interior Designer: Joane Askins, LLC
Landscape Designer: Norman Askins
Antique Building Materials: Wyatt
Childs, Inc.
Plaster: James Galanos
Stucco: I & V Stucco Enterprises, Inc.
Windows and Doors: Asselin, Paris

RURAL ROMANCE

Project Managers: William B. Litchfield
and Greg Harrell
Builder: Tommy D. Baker, Roy Bell
Interior Design: Susan B. Bozeman
Designs, Inc.
Landscape Architect: Edward
Daugherty, Howard Design Studio, LLC
Specialty Finishes: Jill Biskin

FRENCH HISTORY

Project Manager: Hoyte Johnson
Builder: Bonner Custom Homes
Interior Designer: Delores Matich
Landscape Architect: Joe A. Gayle and
Associates
Antique Materials: Alexandria
Sliosberg, Paris
Stair Builder: The Stair Maker, Inc.
Stair Rail: Custom Artisan Group
Stone Fabricator: Cutting Edge Stone
Stonemason: Carlos Rodriguez
Windows and Doors: Asselin, Paris
Post and Beams: Heritage Woodcraft,
Inc.

CLASSICAL GRACE

Project Manager: Ross Piper
Builder: Bonner Custom Homes
Interior Design: Marsden Antiques and
Interiors
Landscape Architect: Howard Design
Studio, LLC
Art Consultant: Ann Kendall Richards,
Inc.
Specialty Finishes: Anne Bielowicz,
Howell Jones
Stair Builder: The Stair Maker, Inc.
Stair Rail: Dillon Forge

DESCANTE

Project Manager: Yong Pak
Builder: Bonner Custom Homes
Landscape Architect: Dargan Landscape
Architects
Antique Materials Consultant: Jean
Pierre Du Bosc, Paris

Steel Doors: Hope's Windows, Inc.
Stucco: I & V Stucco Enterprises, Inc.

THISTLEWAITE

Project Managers: Hoyte Johnson and
Brent Mooneyham
Builder: Tommy Chambers
Interior Designer: Jacquelynne P.
Lanham Designs, Inc., with installation
by Roddy Harris
Landscape Designer: Alex Smith
Antique Materials: Tommy Chambers
Lighting: Edgar-Reeves Lighting &
Antiques

MODERN ENGLISH

Project Managers: David Stoll and
Hoyte Johnson
Builder: Mickey Watkins
Interior Designer: Anne Whitman
Landscape Architect: Richard
Anderson, LA
Antique Materials Consultant: Wyatt
Childs, Inc.
Fine Woods: Atlanta Hardwood
Corporation
Windows and Doors: Asselin, Paris

TROPICAL MERITAGE

Project Manager: Greg Harrell
Builder: Pease Construction
Interior Design: Linda Heagy,
fabrication by Ching Yung, Interior
Dynamics, Chicago
Landscape Architect: Howard Design
Studio, LLC
Decorative Finishes: Anne Bielowicz
Ironwork: Paul ReDavid

FEDERAL FINESSE

Project Manager: Yong Pak
Builder: Rick Bent
Interior Designer: Jacquelynne P.
Lanham Designs, Inc.
Landscape Architect: HighGrove
Partners, LLC
Decorative Finishes: Howell Jones
Furniture Maker: Jim Nugent
Leaded Glass: the late Pat Vloeburgh

SOUTHERN GOTHIC COTTAGE

Project Manager: Jim McConnell
Builder: Neil Gasaway
Interior Designer: Jacquelynne P.
Lanham Designs, Inc.
Landscape Architect: Richard
Anderson, LA

HEIRLOOM HOUSE

Project Manager: Michelle Moody
Builder: Breiding Construction, Inc.
Interior Designer: Susan B. Bozeman
Designs, Inc.
Landscape Architect: Tunnell & Tunnell
Landscape Architecture
Antique Hardware: Monroe Coldren
Decorative Finishes and Specialty Wood
Finishes: Anne Bielowicz
Ironwork: Paul ReDavid

SKY CASTLE

Project Manager: Sheila Rogers
Builder: Joe Stroup
Interior Designer: Owner
Landscape Designer: Owner
Antique Building Materials: Wyatt
Childs, Inc.

CLASSICAL FAMILY HOUSE

Project Manager: William B. Litchfield
Builder: Bonner Custom Homes
Interior Designer: Thom von Buelow,
Lerner-von Buelow
Landscape Architect: Dargan Landscape
Architects
Antique Materials Consultant: Jean
Pierre Du Bosc, Paris
Stair Builder: The Stair Maker, Inc.
Stucco: I & V Stucco Enterprises, Inc.

SOUTHERN CLASSIC

Project Manager: Michelle Moody
Builder: Bonner Custom Homes
Interior Design: Pulliam Morris
Interiors, Columbia, SC
Landscape Architect: Richard
Anderson, LA
Leaded Glass: the late Pat Vloeburgh
Muralist: Christian Thee
Stair Builder: The Stair Maker, Inc.

MEDITERRANEAN ROMANCE

Project Manager: William B. Litchfield
Builder: Webb Builders
Interior Design: Carolyn Malone
Interiors
Landscape Architect: Jorge Sanchez,
Sanchez & Maddux, Inc.
Windows and Doors: Zeluck, Inc.

ACKNOWLEDGMENTS

I dedicate this book to my wife, Joane Lipscomb Askins, for her unerring support and advice throughout its creation. If not for her urging, this work probably would never have become a reality. Joane also graciously assumed the role of innkeeper and chef to entertain Susan Sully on her many photography sessions both in Atlanta and in the mountains. Thanks also go to my daughter, Kathryn Garland Askins, whose support and enthusiasm kept me energized and has meant the world to me. No acknowledgments would be complete without also expressing gratitude for my parents, Elizabeth Davenport and Miller Ross Askins, who were "house people" through and through. My mother instilled in me the love of history, architecture, and all things aesthetic while my father taught me life's lessons about work ethic, being the best you can be, and the importance of always being the perfect Southern gentleman. They gave me and my brother, Ross Askins, unconditional love, encouragement, and support throughout our lives.

Education and internship are two vital aspects of an architect's professional pedigree. I would like to recognize special individuals whose tutelage meant so much to me. James H. Grady, professor of design and history at Georgia Tech, encouraged me to continue my education in architectural history at the University of Virginia, where I studied under William B. O'Neil and Frederick D. Nichols, both of whom expanded my interest and knowledge of classicism. From there, I worked under Paul Buchanan, director of Architectural Research at Colonial Williamsburg, who knew everything about eighteenth-century Virginia architecture and emphasized the importance of primary research. Architect John Milner, with whom I worked in Pennsylvania, was the perfect professional mentor, sharing his knowledge not only of architecture, but also of the business of architecture.

Nothing enhances or diminishes good architecture more than an interior designer. Having attended Parsons summer session during college, I was exposed to the basics, and I've subsequently had the opportunity to collaborate with many fine interior designers, including members of Atlanta's ancien regime, most notably Edith Hills, a style icon then in her nineties, David Byers, Gordon Little, Dotty Travis, and Dan Carithers. Throughout most of my practice I've also worked closely with Nancy Braithwaite and Jacquelynne Lanham, and, more recently, Susan Bozeman. I'm extremely grateful for their collaboration.

I especially want to thank the clients who have entrusted my office to make their dreams a reality over almost four decades. Of these, I have chosen fifteen projects that I feel represent not only some of the best projects, but also illustrate the stylistic breadth of our work. Special thanks go to the clients who graciously allowed their private spaces to be photographed for this book.

I could never have enjoyed my professional success without a great deal of help over the years from the many gifted men and women in my office. For each of them, I am proud and eternally grateful. Each brought their special talent and ability to the office, and some even brought an extra dose of ambition, encouraging me to take on projects I might otherwise have avoided.

I want to especially recognize my office manager, Ginny Lummus. She worked tirelessly coordinating photography sessions, arranging out-of-town trips, typing drafts from my erratic script, and even serving as a photographer's assistant when called upon. Her wit and brains kept us all on track through the entire project.

I would also like to thank The Monacelli Press, especially my editor, Elizabeth White, for taking the leap and agreeing to publish the book, and graphic designer Doug Turshen, who has brought the work to life on the page.

Lastly, I want to give a heartfelt thanks to Susan Sully. It was her initial enthusiasm and many doses of encouragement that pushed me to put my ideas down on paper. Susan spent many hours working with me to get everything right. Top all that off with an excellent photographic eye and you have the makings of a beautiful book. I now count her and her husband, Thomas, as good friends. To Susan, I am eternally grateful for making an idea become a reality.